INSIGHT POCKET GUIDE

CAIRNS

& THE GREAT BARRIER REEF

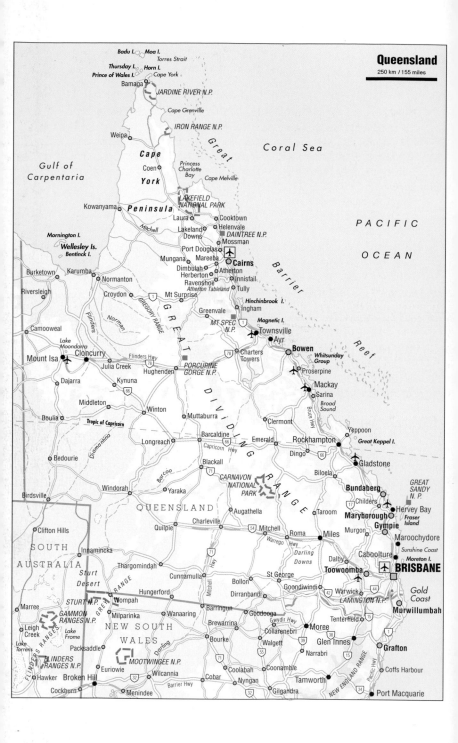

introduction

Welcome

This is one of 133 itinerary-based Pocket Guides produced by the editors of Insight Guides, whose books have set the standard for visual travel guides since 1970. With top-quality photography and authoritative recommendations, this guidebook brings you the very best of Cairns and the Great Barrier Reef in a series of 13 tours devised by Insight's Australia correspondent, Paul Phelan.

Queensland, the sunshine state, is the most visited place in Australia after Sydney. And it is to Cairns, gateway to the Great Barrier Reef, that many visitors are drawn. The city – capital of Tropical North Queensland – has its share of attractions, but its real jewels are found inland and in the cobalt seas bordering it. The first eight itineraries in this guide use Cairns (and nearby beaches like Palm Cove or Port Douglas) as a base to venture into millennia-old rainforests and dramatic plateaus carved by volcanic activity, as well as explore sandy beaches and snorkel on the incredible Great Barrier Reef. This is followed by five excursions to Cape York Peninsula and farther flung beaches and islands: Mission and Airlie beaches, and Dunk, Whitsunday and Heron islands, plus a cruise along the Coral Coast.

Complementing the itineraries in this guide are chapters on outdoor activities, shopping, eating out and nightlife, and a fact-packed practical information section covering all the travel essentials you need to know.

Paul Phelan moved to Queensland more than 30 years ago when he worked as an airline pilot. He moved to Cairns 10 years later, and attracted by Tropical North Queensland's great diversity and natural beauty, and by the earthy good humour and natural friendliness of its people, Phelan soon found himself developing and managing a new holiday resort at the tip of remote Cape York. He is now a full-time writer specialising in travel and aviation.

He is more than amply qualified to act as your guide to this beautiful region along Australia's north-eastern coast: 'I've now flown over, driven across, sailed around or walked over most of the Queensland coastline, and the more I see, the more I find there is waiting to be experienced.' Phelan is also the author of *Insight Pocket Guide Brisbane & the Gold Coast*.

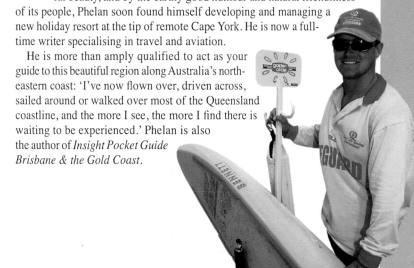

contents   7

LEISURE ACTIVITIES

CALENDAR OF EVENTS

PRACTICAL INFORMATION

MAPS

CREDITS AND INDEX

Pages 2/3: snorkellers, with MV *Reef Endeavour* in the distance
Pages 8/9: picturesque Centenary Lakes in Cairns

History & Culture

Northern Queensland was a late starter in the race to bring European civilisation, culture and economics to Australia. In fact, the process only began about 100 years after the first Europeans settled in the southeast – but Queenslanders say they have achieved the same progress in half the time that it took the rest of the states. The rapidity of Queensland's development has shaped its society and its attitudes, with the celebration of the state's 150th anniversary on 6 June 2009 attracting huge crowds.

Captain Cook's Landing

Historian Gavin Menzies asserts that Chinese fleets sailed to Australia in the early 15th century, making contact with native Australians at more than a dozen places in northern Queensland. However, his claims are widely disputed by other historians.

The voyage of 18th-century maritime explorer Captain James Cook, who sailed up the length of Australia's east coast, was European civilisation's first recorded hint of a vast territory filled with opportunity and promise. Over the previous two centuries, a number of French, Dutch, Portuguese and Spanish navigators landed on the island continent, but they had all approached from the west, encountered arid and inhospitable tracts of coastline, and returned with most unflattering assessments of the land and its native inhabitants.

Returning in 1770 from an expedition to Tahiti, Cook could hardly have chosen a more promising point of first contact on the mainland – on what is now New South Wales' south coast – to begin his northward voyage of exploration. He found a temperate climate, fertile soil, ample water, promising harbours and a population of hunter-gatherers who had never farmed the land but had engaged in extensive burning and clearing of rainforest, turning it into grassy plains, which, ironically, were just what attracted the white invaders/settlers.

To Cook, the maze of coral shoals now known as the Great Barrier Reef were no more than a detested obstacle, which almost robbed him of his ship, his crew and his life. Nor was Cook greeted by inhabitants eager for trade and cultural exchange. Although there is scattered but convincing evidence that earlier civilisations had gained fleeting footholds on the island continent, the only surviving culture when Cook arrived was that of the Aboriginal tribes.

In Pacific Islander legend, when the original Fijians were migrating east from what is now Tanzania in Africa, the only group to escape their marauding raids were the Aborigines of northern Queensland, who cunningly hid until the marauders had passed.

CAPTAIN JAMES COOK
1728 – 1779
COMMANDER H.M.B "ENDEAVOUR"
WHICH WAS BEACHED AND REPAIRED
NEAR THIS SITE 17 JUNE – 4 AUGUST, 1770.
"HE LEFT NOTHING UNATTEMPTED."
THIS STATUE WAS COMMISSIONED BY
BP AUSTRALIA AS A BICENTENNIAL GIFT
TO THE PEOPLE OF COOKTOWN
AND UNVEILED BY MR A W GORRIE
CHAIRMAN OF THE BOARD
SATURDAY, 25 JUNE 1988.
SCULPTOR: STANLEY HAMMOND M.B.E

Left: early European impression of an Aboriginal camp
Right: Captain Cook made his first landing in 1770

In the arid interior, the Aborigines were nomadic because food and water were scarce, and the search for them unrelenting. Along the coast and adjacent ranges, however, the native population was less transient because food and water were more plentiful. The boundaries of these tribal groups were therefore more defined.

Colonisation

Cook claimed the Australian continent in the name of the British Crown, but little was done to develop the land until the War of Independence forced the British to stop shipping convicts to America. As a result, Britain was forced to send its convicts elsewhere, and the place chosen was the land discovered by Captain Cook 17 years previously. The first fleet that sailed into Sydney Cove on 13 May 1787 carried convicts and scarlet-jacketed soldiers rather than settlers, builders or miners, and it was only some years later that the flow of free settlers began.

From Sydney, the newcomers then worked their way northward, and Brisbane, about midway up the east coast, was the last major colonial port to be established – again as a penal colony. Almost the entire Queensland coast therefore remained open for exploration, which began to progress in earnest only after the settlement in the southeast corner was properly established.

The Displaced Aborigines

Queensland's first European settlements were established wherever suitable harbours were found on the coast, to support the agricultural, mining and logging industries of the interior as well as for coastal trading. There is no question that the settlers, miners and explorers showed little regard for Aboriginal feelings, cultures or territorial rights.

Conflicts sprang up endlessly over what the settlers considered to be the theft of their animals and stores by Aborigines. As the European population increased, many Aborigines were marginalised to become fringe dwellers around the settlements, although many proved to be excellent horsemen and livestock handlers.

In 1848, explorer Edmond Kennedy and a party of 12 men landed at Tam O'Shanter Point, near Dunk Island, in search of a way through the ranges behind the coast, intending to travel to the tip of Cape York. His progress was impeded first by swamps and disease, and later on by dis-

Above: Tjapukai performers at the Tjapukai Aboriginal Cultural Park

agreements with Aborigines. Although Kennedy found the inland route less inhospitable than along the densely vegetated and more mountainous east coast, everyone in his party died along the way except one Aboriginal companion. Kennedy himself was fatally speared only miles away from his goal.

On 6 June 1859 Queensland separated from the New South Wales colony, an event now celebrated each year as Queensland Day. Sir George Ferguson Bowen was appointed Queenland's first Governor.

Goldfields and New Seaports

Almost 100 years after Cook's voyage, prospector James Mulligan found gold on the Palmer River in the far north of Queensland, and Cooktown came into being as a seaport and supply link for the new goldfields. In March 1876, gold was also found to the south of the Palmer on the Hodgkinson River, 100km (62 miles) inland, and the need for another port became apparent. Later that year, the mouth of the Bana Bidagarra (now known as the Barron River) was discovered at its outflow into Trinity Bay, where the town of Cairns was established.

The new town of Cairns – named after the then Governor of Queensland, Sir William Wellington Cairns – became a port of entry on 1 November 1876. Once again gold had in a few months brought about developments which would otherwise have taken years. Gold diggers and packers using the Hodgkinson River soon realised they could save 30km (18½ miles) of boggy travel and find good grass for their horses by sailing up the Barron River – until they were stopped by fierce rapids.

A camp was established there; pub and shanty keepers moved in, and soon Smithfield, named after explorer Bill Smith, had a larger population than Cairns. Unfortunately, every time the Barron River flooded, Smithfield became inundated with water. Another reason for its decline was that yet another new port had been established further up the coast, when adventurer and explorer Christie Palmerston discovered an easier route from the coast to the goldfields. The new Port Douglas was declared a port of entry in 1877.

Agriculture and Industry

Sugar cane, rice, timber and cattle were among the first industries to take hold in the region, but as settlements sprang up, prospectors used them as bases from which they found gold and later tin, bauxite, wolfram, copper and other minerals. And in the Torres Strait, pearl shell and *bêche-de-mer*, the sea cucumber prized by the Chinese as a delicacy, were also discovered and exploited.

At first Governor Cairns paid little attention to the tent city carrying his name, but in 1879, after his departure, the first local authority was established in the area, and in 1884 Cairns was declared a municipal borough. A significant event in the town's his-

Right: *The Prospector*, an 1889 painting by Julian Ashton captures the aspirations of the early settlers

tory was the government's decision to build a much-needed railway from the coast to the Atherton Tablelands. Cairns, Gordonvale, Innisfail and Port Douglas all competed for the privilege of having the coastal terminus of the line, but, despite the daunting terrain that would have to be tackled, Cairns won the day. The construction began in 1886, using mainly Italian and Irish workers. A great number of them died from disease and injury, but many more survived and went on to become farmers and businessmen. Notably, many generations of people of Italian descent have dominated the sugar cane industry.

Sugar cane made its first appearance at Cairns in 1881, and a year later, tea and coffee were first planted at Bingil Bay, near Mission Beach. In those early days, the development of such primary industries brought huge demands for labour in the sugar cane fields, as well as to harvest *bêche-de-mer* from the sea, to dive for pearls and to work in the mines.

In times when the law of the jungle prevailed, it was all too easy for some brigand to sail a schooner into the Pacific and force an island chieftain to accept a gallon of rum for his aid in recruiting 'indentured' labour for the cane fields. Large numbers of 'recruited' South Sea Islanders, who came to be known as Kanakas, decided to stay on, and many more returned to work by choice. Likewise, the pearlers and *bêche-de-mer* traders also showed little conscience in their recruitment practices in the Torres Strait and Cape York Peninsula's east coast.

Federation and Conflict

For many Australians, the advent of World War II was the first time Far North Queensland ever came to their notice. The battle of the Coral Sea – the first major carrier-to-carrier naval battle of World War II – which took place from the 4–8 May 1942, was fought between a combined Australian-American force and the Japanese naval and air forces just off the North Queensland coast. Then, in late July 1942, Japanese long-range flying boats raided North Queensland, dropping bombs in the Mossman area, and an imminent invasion seemed to be on the cards. Radar stations were set up, and concealed 'coastwatchers' were positioned along the coast to Cape York. Atherton's Barron Valley Hotel was used as headquarters for part of the war and thousands of troops were camped in the area for jungle warfare training.

Fortunately, the Japanese invasion never materialised, but a memorial erected by the only person injured in the bombing, Carmel Emmi (née Zollo) and unveiled on the 50th anniversary of the bombing, can be seen near the town of Mossman.

Above: Pacific islanders labouring in the cane fields of the Queensland coast, circa 1900
Right: the Great Barrier Reef, accursed by sailors in Cook's day, is a treasured asset today

Post-War Development

Two world wars and more than 130 years of high-volume settlement by diverse groups of migrants from Europe and Asia have helped develop Cairns into a thriving tropical city, with an economy based on tourism and the sugar, mining and dairy industries. In the first half of the 20th century there was little recognition of the potential offered by the Great Barrier Reef, which stretches some 2,300km (1,430 miles) along the Queensland coast. Instead, it was regarded as a nuisance to shipping, with more than 1,600 shipwrecks recorded. Now, however, safe routes and a shipping pilot service provide safe passage for the transit of merchant ships and countless fishing and pleasure vessels.

The reef and the region's tropical coastline and hinterland have become major tourist attractions. No longer are rainforests something to be torn down for timber and the land exploited for agriculture; and no longer is the Great Barrier Reef nothing but a navigation hazard and an unlimited source of delicious seafood.

Growth of Tourism

Cairns Airport was upgraded to receive international flights in 1984, and became the major hub for Australian Airlines, which flew to many overseas airports, including Tokyo, Osaka and Kota Kinabalu. Sadly, the demise of the airline in 2006 led to a decline in the relative importance of Cairns as an international air-hub; however, Jestar has stepped in to fill, at least partially, the gap left by the departure of Australian Airlines. There are now international flights from Cairns to Auckland, Tokyo, Hong Kong, Guam, Port Moresby and Singapore (via Darwin).

As the centre of tourist activity in the area, Cairns has largely been taken over by high-rise hotels and shopping malls, but you can still find fine examples of traditional buildings made from the wood of cedar and silky oak trees. The advent of electric fans and air conditioning, and the increasing price and scarcity of timber, have since transformed construction, but some of the trademarks, such as timber lattice, have survived in modern buildings, imparting a distinctive Queensland architectural style.

But there have been ecological disasters too. In 1935, cane toads were introduced into the Gordonvale area south of Cairns from Hawaii in order to combat the sugar cane beetle which was destroying precious cane crops. The beetle, however, inhabited the flowers and seeds 1.8m (6ft) above the ground and beyond the reach of the terrestrial cane toad, which has now hopped all over Queensland and become a pest in about half of Australia, In March 2009 the first government-sponsored 'Toad Day Out' was organised, when hundreds of local people went hunting for the invasive creature, catching around 10,000 toads which were then humanely killed.

Melting Pot

The region's lawless past is behind it, and its natural beauty and economic strength have assured its future. Queensland's population is now 3.6 million, with more than 20 percent of Cairns' 140,000 population born overseas. Indigenous languages are almost as culturally diverse as the population, while the Italian- and Greek-speaking communities make up two of the largest and oldest population groups in the region. Polish, Spanish, Croatian, Dutch, German, Russian, Swiss and South Americans are fewer in number but significantly represented.

Cairns also has a growing refugee community from the former Yugoslavia, Sudan, West Papua and Iraq. South Pacific Islander groups from Papua New Guinea, East Timor, Fiji, the Cook Islands, Samoa, Tonga and Maori New Zealanders are among the fastest growing language groups, while there is also significant immigration from Japan, Malaysia, India and Indonesia.

The intermingling of cultures has enriched every aspect of the region's culture – which is nowhere more evident than in the markets that flourish at all major (and many minor) centres, in the range and diversity of city restaurants, and in the variety of its places of religious worship. At the same time, the flow of internal migrants from the southern states of Australia, as well as those from from other countries, continues unabated.

Above: Pacific Islander immigrants weaving a mat at Fogarty Park, Cairns

HISTORY HIGHLIGHTS

1770 Captain James Cook explores Australia's east coast.

1787 The first fleet sails into Sydney Cove on 13 May, loaded with convicts and marines.

1802 Explorer Matthew Flinders in HMS *Investigator* sails through the Whitsunday Passage and charts the inner edge of the Great Barrier Reef.

1825 A convict settlement is established on the site of Brisbane, now the state capital.

1848 Edmund Kennedy sets out from Tam O'Shanter Point to chart a land route up the Cape York Peninsula.

1864 The Jardine brothers set out from the Burnett region to drive a herd of cattle and horses to the tip of remote Cape York.

1868 Queensland's pearling industry is established in the Torres Straits.

1873 James Mulligan discovers payable gold on the Palmer River and receives an award of £1,000 from the government.

1876 Gold is found on the Hodgkinson River. A party reaches Trinity Bay and the new town of Cairns is proclaimed a port of entry to serve the mining industry from Trinity Inlet.

1877 Adventurer Christie Palmerston discovers an easier route from the goldfields to the coast, and Port Douglas is declared a port of entry.

1882 Tea and coffee are for the first time planted at Bingil Bay, and sugar cane at Gordonvale.

1884 Cairns is declared a municipal borough.

1885 Legislation is passed to discontinue the 'recruiting' of Pacific islanders for Queensland's tropical agriculture, to be implemented over the next five years.

1891 The Cairns to Kuranda railway line is completed.

1896 The first sugar cane is crushed at the Mulgrave Central Mill at Gordonvale, south of Cairns.

1901 Australia's six independent colonies are federated into the Commonwealth of Australia under a common constitution.

1920 Passenger ships offer one-day stopovers on a Whitsunday 'tropical island', heralding the area's success as a tourism destination.

1926 The Cairns to Yungaburra range road (now Gillies Highway) is opened.

1929 The first Whitsunday resort is established on Lindeman Island.

1942 Japanese planes attack Pearl Harbor in the USA and later Darwin. Australian naval bases are established at Cairns and Thursday Island. The Battle of the Coral Sea is fought. Catalina flying boats operating from Cairns attack Japanese positions in the Pacific.

1947 Airline owner Reg Ansett introduces big business into the Whitsundays with acquisition of Hayman Island.

1951 Bush Pilots Airways, established to open up communications and transport on Cape York, makes its first scheduled flight.

1984 Cairns International Airport is opened. A track, negotiable only by off-road vehicles, is opened up between Cape Tribulation and Bloomfield River amid considerable protest.

1988 World Heritage status is accorded to 900,000ha (2¼ million acres) of North Queensland's tropical rainforests.

1992 Australian High Court rejects the *Terra Nullus* (empty land) concept that had existed since the time of European discovery, and rules that native title has survived the annexation of the country.

2001 Australian Federation Centenary.

2003 Development of Cairns foreshore as a centre of visitor leisure activity is completed.

2006 Cyclone Larry, one of the worst natural disasters on record, devastates Innisfail district. First all-weather road brings reliable access to Cooktown.

2008 Formation of Cairns Regional Council. Val Schier sworn in as mayor in April, taking over from long-serving mayor Kevin Byrne.

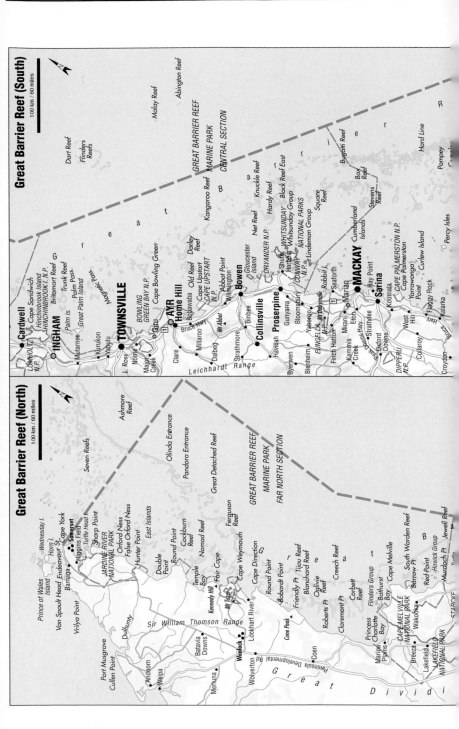

Great Barrier Reef (South)

100 km / 60 miles

GREAT BARRIER REEF MARINE PARK CENTRAL SECTION

Great Barrier Reef (North)

100 km / 60 miles

GREAT BARRIER REEF MARINE PARK FAR NORTH SECTION

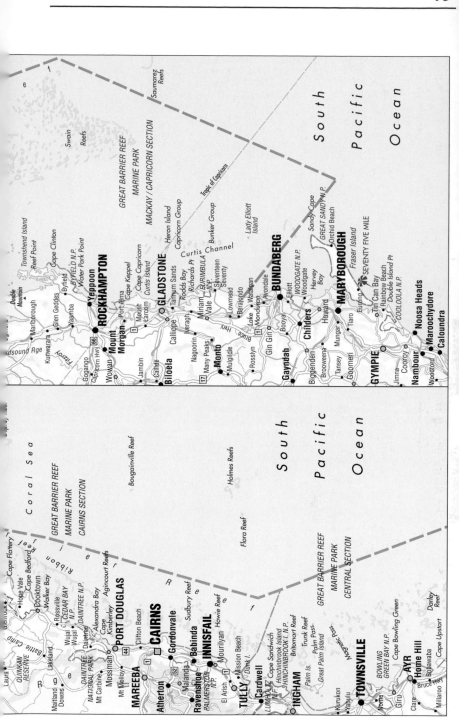

orientation

Orientation

Tropical North Queensland occupies the far northeast corner of Australia, and its greatest treasures are the Great Barrier Reef and the Wet Tropics rainforest – both designated by Unesco as World Heritage Sites. The Great Barrier Reef – which includes some 2,900 individual reefs, 300 coral cays and more than 1,000 islands – spans over 350,000sq km (135,000sq miles) in area. It stretches for 2,300km (1,430 miles) off the east coast of Queensland in the aptly named Coral Sea, and up here in the Tropical North is where it is closest to the shore. Some 80km (50 miles) wide in places, the reef and its coral islands form a wonderland of marine life. And along the mainland shore is a succession of white-sand beaches backed by lush rainforest.

Stretching back from the coast, and extending for over 9,000sq km (3,500sq miles), the Wet Tropics rainforest is the oldest of its kind in the world, and with the greatest diversity of endemic species. Further south, rolling inland towards the Great Dividing Range, are the Cairns Highlands, also known as the Atherton Tablelands, with fertile pastures and cattle stations, country towns, and scenic lakes and waterfalls. And beyond this lies the Outback and the old mining settlements.

Cairns, on Trinity Bay, is perfectly placed for exploring everything the Tropical North has to offer, both on and offshore. Backed by forested hills, it's a compact town right on the main coastal highway, with most of the action found around the Esplanade area. One thing to remember if you're coming from the northern hemisphere is that the seasons are in reverse here – Christmas is in mid-summer – and the orientation is opposite, with the water spiralling down the plug-hole the opposite way.

Cairns, Palm Cove or Port Douglas?

This book contains eight itineraries, each occupying a whole day, followed by five excursions for longer trips (including a cruise), which incorporate overnight stops along the way. Cairns is the most obvious choice as a base for a North Queensland holiday because it has the main transport links, including an international airport, railway and long-distance bus connections, along with a plethora of holiday accommodation, nightlife, restaurants and shopping outlets.

But because of this, Cairns has become rather built-up and can be boisterous – and it doesn't have a beach – so you may prefer to base yourself at Palm Cove, Port Douglas, Mission Beach or other beachside resorts along the Tropical North Queensland coast. Wherever you stay, you will need to hire a car (possibly a four-wheel-drive) for the trips in this guide, except Excursions 4 and 5, to which you will be flying.

Left: Kuranda Scenic Railway on Stony Creek bridge
Right: the always adorable koala

1. EXPLORING CAIRNS *(see map below)*

A coastal and rainforest walk with tropical scenery and elevated views across the city, taking in the Esplanade, Botanic Gardens, Tanks Art Centre and Royal Flying Doctor Service Visitor Centre.

Start at the pathway opposite the Sofitel Reef Casino on the seafront side of the Hilton Hotel. You could get around this itinerary in half a day, but it can more comfortably fill a whole day or longer. If you want to break and then resume the route, buses run hourly from the Lake Street Transit Hub in the city centre to the Botanical Gardens. If it's too hot or wet, or if your time is limited, you could spend a rewarding half day on horticulturalist Andrew Doolan's Cairns Discovery Tour (City Sights Plus; tel: 07 4053 5259; www.cairnsdiscoverytours.com).

From the boardwalk along the sea wall you'll see dozens of yachts and powered craft moored in the enclosed marina and along the opposite shore, many occupied by people who have sailed into Cairns en route to somewhere else, become addicted to the city's relaxed lifestyle, and decided to stay on. Opposite the boardwalk, a chain of restaurants and cafés offers refreshments – but note that high rents on The Esplanade push café prices way up.

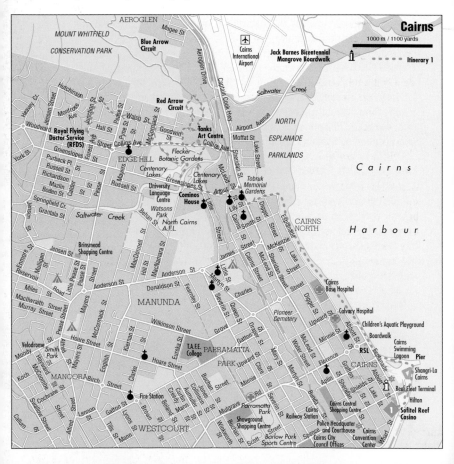

The Esplanade Area

Keep to the shoreline path to the right of the hotel and the **Pier** complex, overlooking the marina. Around the corner you'll find a huge, usually crowded, landscaped swimming lagoon, with a walkway along the sea wall. This area, and the rest of the **Esplanade**, including an aquatic children's playground, is the hub of Cairns' activities and a window on its relaxed lifestyle.

Much of the coastal parkland is on reclaimed ground. At high tide, the water laps the narrow beach all the way along the shoreline, and that's when the brochure photographs are taken. When it recedes, Cairns' famous and not unattractive mud flats are exposed. The mud, dumped during World War II when the shipping channel was dredged, has spread across the bay's shallows and is rich in marine life. This has created a new home for hundreds of water birds, some of which migrate from as far away as Siberia.

A major upgrade of The Esplanade was completed in late 2006, with the opening of the North Esplanade Parklands, marked by a distinctive concrete dome topped by a galvanised iron 'cockatoo's crest', and incorporating a skate park, bike path and extensive lawns and gardens. The walking path now extends as far as the airport.

Indigenous Vegetation

At the northern end of the pathway you'll have walked about 4km (2½ miles). Pass behind the children's playground ship and continue along the parallel Esplanade for another block, turn left, and when you reach the sports ground a block further on, walk diagonally across it (unless the hockey sticks are flying) to pass the Tobruk Pool on your right. At the lights, cross Sheridan Street into Arthur Street, which becomes Greenslopes Street after a couple of blocks, then go over the railway crossing and Lily Creek bridge. On the next corner is **Cominos House**, a typical colonial-style home built on stilts, that was the residence of one of Cairns' earliest settler families until 1988. Relocated from its original Abbot Street site, it has been adapted to form an environmental and arts centre.

Opposite the house is a foot and cycle path into the **Cairns Botanical Gardens**, which consist of four main areas: the main gardens (Flecker Botanical Gardens; Mon–Fri 7.30am–5.30pm; Sat–Sun and public holidays 8.30am–5.30pm; tel: 07 4044 3098); **Centenary Lakes**; **Mount Whitfield Conservation Park** and the **Australian Gondwanan Heritage Garden**.

Above: the Esplanade's sprawling swimming lagoon
Right: tranquil Centenary Lakes

You are first treated to a shady park with a small saltwater lake to your left, a waterfowl habitat that is well worth a pause. This area is a tidied-up version of the original countryside, with predominantly native trees typical of the vegetation of low-lying coastal land in the region. From a footbridge across the mangrove-lined **Saltwater Creek**, try to imagine the daunting environment that first challenged early explorers who ventured up the hostile, crocodile-infested waterway by boat.

The Red Arrow Walk

You'll soon emerge onto Collins Avenue opposite the **Tanks Art Centre**, converted wartime fuel tanks that are now used as premises for temporary art exhibitions, usually with local themes. Opening hours vary, so call 07 4032 6600 for information.

Walk along Collins Avenue to a small off-street parking bay on the right, which is the beginning of the 1.3-km (0.8-mile) **Red Arrow Walk**. A well-made but steep walking track leads you to tranquil gullies, through virgin rainforest, and to sweeping viewpoints that look out over the town centre, Trinity Bay, the airport, and the mangrove creeks and swamps along the coastline. When you come to a fork in the track, take the left path – the walk goes around a loop from this point, returning down the other path. At the top of the ridge, take the right fork (the left one is the more strenuous 5.4-km/3.4-mile Blue Arrow circuit) and along the spur you'll find a covered shelter overlooking the airport – a great place to rest awhile and enjoy the scenery. On the return path there are fine views of the city.

Back at the car park, turn right up Collins Avenue and in a few hundred metres you'll reach the **Botanic Gardens** proper. The **Botanic Gardens Restaurant** (daily 7am–4pm; tel: 07 4053 7087) in the grounds is ideally placed for a coffee/tea break or for lunch. A good range of wines and beer is also available.

Suitably refreshed, take some time to wander through the more formal part of the gardens, which are rich in both indigenous and exotic species. At the gardens' office, pick up a walk leaflet or an audio-tour (in several languages). The gardens contain most of the timber species that first drew the white population to Cairns, including Queensland cedar and several varieties of silky oak, which polishes to a hologram-like finish and forms the structure of many of the older homes.

Above: signage, Tanks Arts Centre
Left: palm fruit at the Botanic Gardens
Right: mural, Royal Flying Doctor Service

Flying Doctor Service

From the gardens, walk up McCormack Street, which runs off Collins Avenue to the west, and turn left into Walsh Street. Here you can catch some fascinating glimpses of what became the city's first 'upper-crust' suburb, **Edge Hill**, where much of its distinctive architectural style developed. Turn left again into Junction Street, and on your right just before the street bends to the left, you'll arrive at the interesting **Royal Flying Doctor Service Visitors' Centre** (Mon–Sat 9am–4.30pm; tel: 07 4053 5687; www.flyingdoctor.org.au).

More than 80 years ago, Dr John Flynn, a missionary in the remote interior, saw a need to bring modern health and emergency medical services to what was then the far-flung Outback. Using vintage planes and primitive communications based on pedal-driven radios, the Flying Doctor Service became a vital link between the Outback and the major population centres, bringing health care and emergency medical services to remote communities. The service is provided free to those who need it, and paid for by government grants and private and corporate donations. The sense of community that the service helped to enhance is one of the most inspiring stories of Australia's inland development. You can see a 15-minute video at the centre, 'A Day in the Life of the Flying Doctor', which brings the story to life.

Back on the road, it's just a short walk around the corner and along Fleming Street, and a right turn takes you to the Edge Hill roundabout.

Walk back along Collins Avenue to the Botanic Gardens and take the path opposite the main entrance, which leads to the **Rainforest Boardwalk**. This elevated walkway keeps your feet dry as you pass through otherwise untouched lowland rainforest, with its giant paperbark trees (whose official name is *Melaleuca quinquenervia*), pandanus and indigenous palm species. At the end of the boardwalk, fringing the Melaleuca Wetlands, is a freshwater lake, its surface adorned with waterlilies. When you've seen enough, the best way to return to the central business district is by the way you came – along the Esplanade.

2. PORT DOUGLAS AND MOSSMAN GORGE
(see map, below & p28)

Sail and swim or just take it easy on the famous Four Mile Beach at the chic resort of Port Douglas, then explore scenic Mossman Gorge.

Wherever you are based, the Captain Cook Highway will bring you to the Port Douglas turn-off. From Cairns you need to go north past the Smithfield roundabout and continue for 64km (40 miles), taking a right turn onto Port Douglas Road. As the road curves left, turn right into Barrier Street for the south end of Four Mile Beach. Bring swimming gear, mosquito repellent and sun protection.

Not very long ago, **Port Douglas** was a sleepy seaside settlement. Today, it has been transformed into a fashionable and up-market tropical holiday resort and retirement township, with the whole spectrum of tourist accommodation and attendant diversions. Fortunately, the transition has not robbed Port Douglas of its natural charms.

The approach from the main road is an early clue to the town's evolution. It is lined by an avenue of about 450 huge African oil palms, and as many again are planted around the Sheraton Mirage Resort and the Marina Mirage – part of the extravagant vision of former multi-millionaire Christopher Skase, who went spectacularly bust in a series of Australian and international media and leisure ventures. About 1,500 palm trees were transplanted here in the

Above: Port Douglas' famous Four Mile Beach

Map labels:

Port Douglas
1000 m / 1100 yards

Island Point
Magazine Island
Dickson Inlet
Macrossan St
Mowbray St
Marina Mirage
Lookout Point
Port Douglas Water Sports
Port St
Davidson St
Packers Creek
CORAL
FOUR
Port Douglas Road
Sheraton Mirage Resort
SEA
Golf Course
MILE
Golf Course
Golf Course
Mossman
Trinity Bay
Captain Cook Hwy
Rainforest Habitat Wildlife Sanctuary
Cairns
Golf Course
Craiglie

mid-1980s at a cost of about AU$1,500 each. Happily, Port Douglas fared better than its benefactor, and the town has continued to survive and prosper.

Four Mile Beach

Four Mile Beach is the prime asset of Port Douglas. Funnily enough the beach is only 4km (2½ miles) long. It was named after an Aboriginal lady known as 'Four Mile'. Once backed by nothing but hinterland swamp, it still retains an air of spacious solitude – unless you peer through the bush and discover cabanas where crocodiles once lurked. Take the pathway near the southern end of the beach, the least crowded part, where the temptation might be to simply crash out on the sands and soak up the sun – or you could stroll the 4km (2½ miles) to the northern end (and maybe get a taxi back). Swimming is safe, but stay inside the nets in the stinger season (these nasty box jellyfish infest the waters offshore from October to May). Another possibility is to hire a catamaran, sea kayak or double surf skis (Port Douglas Water Sports; Mar–Nov daily 9am–5pm, weather permitting; tel: 0404 856 821), and test your skill at skimming the blue water.

Next, get back in the car and retrace your route to Port Douglas Road, turning right for the drive up to the 'central business district', where souvenir and beach fashion shops compete for your attention and your dollars. Browse for a while, then drive to the parkland fronting the water. Turn right up Wharf Street, a steep hill containing some of Port Douglas' most expensive residences, to reach **Lookout Point**. From here, there are sweeping views over Four Mile Beach and the coastline, extending most of the way to Cairns and the mountains beyond. You can also see Skase's centrepiece, now the **Sheraton Mirage Resort** and **Marina Mirage**, the boating-cum-shopping complex he built on reclaimed mangrove swamp.

For a delicious lunch, get an outside table at the waterside seafood restaurant, **On The Inlet** (3 Inlet Street; tel: 07 4099 5255), where most of the seafood is local – try the warm prawn carpaccio.

Mossman Gorge and the Rainforest Sanctuary

Drive back down Wharf Street and take the main road south from Port Douglas to meet Captain Cook Highway. You pass the Rainforest Habitat Wildlife Sanctuary, but keep going – we'll return here later. At the main road turn right, and it's only a 21-km (13-mile) drive north to Mossman. Turn left here and follow the signs for another 5km (3 miles) to **Mossman Gorge**, passing through sugar cane fields and later rainforest to reach the **Mossman River**.

From the car park here, you can access the swimming area a little way upstream, either along a well-made path through the bush or an only slightly less easy one along the river bank beside the roaring rapids. Swimming in the cool, clear water among the rocks is safe, but excercise caution. Just a little further up the path is a suspension bridge leading to a 2½-km (1½-mile) walking circuit through the rainforest, with interpretive signs detailing many of the plant

Right: Mossman River Gorge

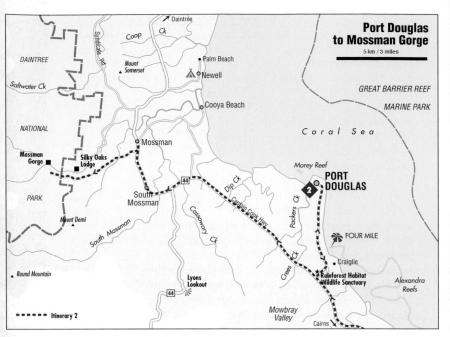

Port Douglas to Mossman Gorge
5 km / 3 miles

species growing there, and how they are used by the Aboriginal Kuku Yalanji people and various forest animals.

When you have seen enough, head back towards Port Douglas; just after turning off the Captain Cook Highway, look for signs on the left for the **Rainforest Habitat Wildlife Sanctuary** (daily 8am–5.30pm; tel: 07 4099 3235; www.rainforesthabitat.com.au), which offers a chance to observe up close some 180 species of flora and fauna in four environments: rainforest, wetlands, woodlands and grasslands. The outdoor 'Breakfast with the Birds' (daily 8–10.30am) experience is very popular. In the rainforest you'll see native species such as Boyd's forest dragon, eclectus parrots, red-tailed black cockatoos and green tree frogs, in a natural setting. A meandering walkway allows you to experience different levels of the rainforest from ground to high in the canopy. In the wetlands, wading birds can be seen foraging for fish and crustacea in waterways that wind beneath boardwalks and pathways, while the grasslands introduce you to a range of macropods, from the statuesque Eastern Grey kangaroo to the petite Parma wallaby.

The billabong is home to turtles, frogs and a range of waterfowl while also attracting a host of native birds; over 40 species using the area for breeding have been recorded. Estuarine and freshwater crocodiles lurk beneath the murky waters or bask on the sunlit banks. Last is the koala habitat, which provides visitors with an eye-level view of this unusual marsupial.

Hartley's Crocodile Adventures (Wangeti Beach; tel: 07 4055 3576) provides a great opportunity to get to know (not *too* closely) crocodiles and other wildlife, with expert guides on hand to explain all you ever wanted to know, and more. A major new attraction is **Gondwana Gateway**, a timeline and 'evolutionary walk' through 17 million years of natural history.

3. KURANDA SCENIC CIRCUIT *(see map, p32)*

Travel to picturesque Kuranda on the Scenic Railway, buy souvenirs from hippies-turned-capitalists, and return to Cairns on the Skyrail cable car, skimming tropical rainforest and waterfalls along the way.

Get to Cairns Central Station in time to catch the 8.30am train (which also stops at Freshwater station at 8.45am). Book the rail and cableway package with Skyrail (tel: 07 4038 1555; www.skyrail.com.au). You'll also need to decide on a departure time from Kuranda – 2 or 2.30pm will give you plenty of time at the Skyrail stops. Bring a camera and binoculars, wear comfortable shoes, and for reasons you'll discover later, a bright red, pink or white shirt or blouse if you have one.

Don't be put off by anything but continuous heavy rain, because the rainforest can be at its most fascinating when shrouded in mist – and rainfall increases the number and the spectacle of the waterfalls. The journeys in both directions are as enjoyable as the destination. Outwards you will be travelling in 100-year-old railway carriages, which are carefully maintained and refurbished by Queensland Rail, on the **Kuranda Scenic Railway** (tel: 07 4036 9333; www.ksr.com.au).

When you book, ask for a seat about mid-train (it gets quite noisy at the front) or opt for the Royale Service (in 'Gold Class'), where for a little more money, you'll enjoy a refreshing glass of bucks fizz, a fancy name for champagne and orange juice, and a personal guide. Note: there are open-air verandas at each end of some cars for close-to-nature viewing.

A Scenic Ride

The train trundles to Freshwater to pick up more passengers, then continues through the sugar cane fields around Redlynch on Cairns' outer fringe before it climbs up the side of the steep mountain range overlooking the **Barron River Gorge**. The wheels squeal as the track winds into the gullies and around the ridges, with no fewer than 15 tunnels along the way.

A commentary on the railway's construction reminds you of the immensity of the engineering task faced by the predominantly Irish and Italian workforce, who hacked the trackbed out of solid rock with hand tools, buckets and bare hands, aided in the toughest places by dynamite.

The train slows down as it crosses **Stony Creek bridge** over a steep gully, with a backdrop of one of the region's most spectacular waterfalls. Here, pause to think about the obstacles faced by the construction workers – heavy rain that caused flooding and landslides, and appalling conditions spreading disease

Left: Barron Falls becomes a trickle in the dry season

itineraries

in the base camps. At least 23 workers died before the railway opened up the rich Atherton Tablelands to agriculture and later to tourism. At a brief photo stop at the station overlooking **Barron Falls**, see the river plunge (or trickle, depending on the time of year) from its placid Kuranda reaches and into the gorge.

Kuranda Markets

At the **Kuranda Railway Station**, which you'll reach after 10am, there's a free bus to the village – don't think about walking because it's uphill and you'll cover the same ground walking back to the Skyrail terminal. Most of the village's attractions are attuned to the rail schedules and open from 10am to 4pm, so individual hours will only be included where they differ.

Kuranda village is less than 1km (½ mile) from end to end. It was 'discovered' in the 1960s by hippies who wanted to live in idyllic surroundings, well away from streamlined civilisation, where the occasional recreational smoke (and cultivating the necessary foliage) wouldn't raise an eyebrow. In the 1980s, a sternly disapproving Queensland government took strong action against several North Queensland alternative lifestyle colonies, and one alleged illicit horticulturalist was actually shot while fleeing a dawn raid.

The rainforest setting also attracted a colony of talented artists and craftspeople. The 'original' **Kuranda Markets**, which trade from Wednesdays to Fridays and on Sundays, from 9am to 3pm, sell a cheerful jumble of local and imported crafts and produce, while diagonally across the road at the more commercial **Heritage Markets** (daily 9.30am–3.30pm; tel: 07 4093 8060), a range of mostly local craft work is offered. Just outside, you'll see a 'crashed' airliner – a vintage DC-3 formerly used as a film prop – swathed in jungle vegetation.

Above: bustling scene, Kuranda Markets
Left: indigenous kookaburra at Birdworld Kuranda

Birds and Butterflies

At the rear of the market a red-tailed black cockatoo or a pink and grey galah stand sentinel just outside **Birdworld Kuranda** (daily 9am–4pm; admission charge; tel: 07 4093 9188; www.birdworldkuranda.com). You can step into the enclosure and stroll among more than 500 free-flying birds of 55 native and 24 exotic species, including the cassowary, an endangered denizen of North Queensland's rainforests. The birds are tame and friendly, and it's quite common to have a colourful Eclectus parrot or one of its fellow inmates land on your shoulder during the half-hour or more you're likely to spend there. If you stay completely motion-less they are more likely to come to you.

Close by, the **Australian Butterfly Sanctuary** (daily 9.45am–4pm; admission charge; tel: 07 4093 7575; www.australianbutterflies.com) is home to about 2,000 of these enchanting creatures, with nearly a dozen native species fluttering among the foliage. It's an all-weather attraction, being under cover. The butterflies are reared in the sanctuary, not taken from the wild, so they are not the least bit timid – and if you took my early advice and wore something bright red, pink or white, they are more likely to land on you for a closer inspection. The two prettiest butterflies are the dazzling blue and black Ulysses (attracted to pink, the colour of its favourite flower) and the golden green Cairns Birdwing. **Birdworld Kuranda**, **Australian Butterfly Sanctuary** and **Koala Gardens** (Rob Veivers Drive; tel: 07 4093 9953) are connected by a walkway, and a single discounted ticket covers all three of these attractions.

Aim to have lunch after 12.30pm, when the coach tour crowds will have moved on. Kuranda isn't short of places to eat and the competition is reflected in both choice and quality. Try the timber-clad, semi-alfresco **Frogs Restaurant** (11 Coondoo Street; tel: 07 4093 7405); sit at the rear where there is usually a breeze, and order the delicious grilled barramundi. After lunch, it's all downhill through Kuranda's very commercialised but still creative main street. Among the landmarks you'll pass en route to the Skyrail are two pubs, known unimaginatively as the **Top Pub** and the **Bottom Pub** – or maybe you won't just pass them if you have worked up a thirst.

Skyrail through the Rainforest

You will have a pre-booked time to arrive at the **Skyrail Rainforest Cableway** (tel: 07 4038 1555; www.skyrail.com.au) for the return trip. Each Skyrail gondola has a sweeping 360-degree view and the full complement of six passengers is not unduly limiting (outside the highest season, you'll normally have only a short wait to get one to yourselves). Back in 1993–4, eco-activist Manfred Stevens spent 202 days in a tree under the current Skyrail route. 'I'm going to stop this project at any cost!', he said. But stop it he didn't – and today, conservation groups and high-profile visitors, including the son of

Right: sweep across the rainforest canopy on the Skyrail

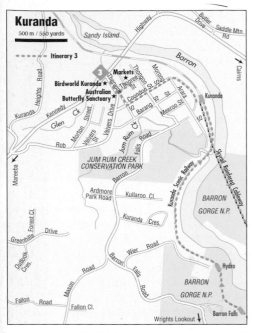

Jacques Cousteau, have added their accolades to the Skyrail service. As you set off, skimming across the Barron River, you see Kuranda and its surrounding rainforest from another perspective. Then you are within a few metres of the rainforest canopy, where you can see the multiple layers that make up its complex ecosystems.

Boardwalk Lookouts

In about 10 minutes you've reached the **Barron Falls** station, where you disembark onto a boardwalk that takes you to two lookouts commanding unforgettable forest-framed views of the falls, especially impressive when the Barron is in full flood.

Here, the efficient **Rainforest Interpretive Centre** has also provided high-tech interactive displays, videos and useful information. Skyrail's next leg sweeps you over more rainforest to **Red Peak**, where you transfer onto a second cableway – the distance being too great for a single cable. At this stop, take advantage of the complimentary ranger-guided walks (every 20 minutes) on walkways just above the forest floor. Back at the Skyrail terminal in Cairns, a low-cost coach will take you back to the railway station to pick up your car, or to your Cairns hotel.

4. TJAPUKAI, PALM COVE AND CAIRNS TROPICAL ZOO
(see pull-out map)

A day that combines a look at Aboriginal art and culture, a bit of lazing on the beach and some exciting wildlife experiences at a tropical zoo.

Although the Tjapukai is right next to the Skyrail terminal in Cairns, I've elected not to combine this attraction with Itinerary 3 as it's too much to do in a single day. Try and get to Tjapukai by 9am. If you're travelling down from a base further north, take the Captain Cook Highway to Smithfield, then follow the signs for Skyrail. Bring swimwear and sun protection for the beach.

At the **Tjapukai Aboriginal Cultural Park** (daily 9am–5pm; admission charge; tel: 07 4042 9999; www.tjapukai.com.au), the 'story of the Tjapukai people' uses new technology to tell the ancient story of the local Aborigines preserving and presenting their traditional culture. The languages of the local Djabugay and Yirrgandji peoples are now being taught to both Aboriginal and white children in Cairns schools. Headset commentaries in eight languages are available in two of the five theatres. The park re-opens at 7pm for dinner and an interactive three-act show four times a week (Tues, Thur, Fri and Sun).

All the plants in the 25-ha (57-acre) site are native to the area, and some of them provided the traditional food of the Aborigines. As well as the high-tech exhibits, there are demonstrations, including instruction in boomerang and spear throwing, how to light a fire without matches and to play the dijeridu (didgeridoo), the traditional wind instrument of the Aborigines. You can also watch a bush medicine show, and there is a restaurant offering specialities like emu burgers and crocodile hot dogs.

You might want to make a short detour first, turning west at the first roundabout north of Smithfield and up McGregor Road to visit the **A J Hackett Bungy Jumping** (daily 9.30am–5pm; tel: 07 4057 7188) tower and watch enthusiasts hurl themselves from the 50-m (164-ft) tower.

Palm Cove Beach

Otherwise, head north on the Captain Cook Highway for about 15 minutes towards Palm Cove, stopping off at Cairns Tropical Zoo on the way to pick up their leaflet detailing the programme of afternoon events – study this at your leisure on the beach and make plans for later.

Palm Cove, the largest of the northern beach resort areas before Port Douglas, is where many visitors base themselves. Unlike Cairns, it has a beach, and a nice one too, with waters that are deeper than at other beaches further south, making it clearer in choppy weather. You can rent a catamaran here, or try your hand at windsurfing. If you just want to relax on the sands and you like seclusion, take a walk along the very long beach until you get beyond the halfway point, where there are few buildings (you may also notice some relaxation of beachwear formality). If you keep walking it becomes populated again at **Clifton Beach**.

Left: Kuranda sightseers taking a break
Above: experience the aboriginal culture through the eyes of a Tjapukai

Palm Cove also has a deep water jetty, where you'll usually find dozens of locals and visitors trying to prove they're smarter than the fish; the measure of their success is to be found in their plastic buckets – which are often empty.

When you're ready for lunch, enjoy an alfresco meal overlooking the beach at **Far Horizons** (Angsana Resort & Spa, 1 Veivers Road; tel: 07 4055 3000). The menu is rich in local seafood and produce from the market gardens of the Cairns Highlands. Or spoil yourself at the **Reef House Restaurant** at the luxury Sebel Reef House hotel (99 Williams Esplanade; tel: 07 4055 3633), where subtle Asian flavours enhance the seafood, beef and chicken, and there are superb beach or pool views.

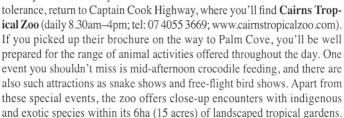

Tropical Zoo

When you've reached your suntan tolerance, return to Captain Cook Highway, where you'll find **Cairns Tropical Zoo** (daily 8.30am–4pm; tel: 07 4055 3669; www.cairnstropicalzoo.com). If you picked up their brochure on the way to Palm Cove, you'll be well prepared for the range of animal activities offered throughout the day. One event you shouldn't miss is mid-afternoon crocodile feeding, and there are also such attractions as snake shows and free-flight bird shows. Apart from these special events, the zoo offers close-up encounters with indigenous and exotic species within its 6ha (15 acres) of landscaped tropical gardens.

After this, head back down to Cairns for the evening. Nearby are Cairns Night Zoo and The Opal Cave and Opal Theatre. You can stroll around the Esplanade's **Night Markets** (daily 4.30–11pm), maybe choose a pearl right out of the oyster *(see Shopping, page 77)* and get an inexpensive meal from one of the 14 international outlets within the market. For a more up-market meal on The Esplanade, choose between Australian-style seafood at the **Raw Prawn** (103 The Esplanade; tel: 07 4031 5400), Chinese at **Café China** (Rydges Plaza

Complex, corner of Spence Street and Grafton Street; tel: 07 4441 2828) and Italian cuisine at **Villa Romana Trattoria** (corner of Esplanade and Aplin Street; tel: 07 4051 9000; www.villaromana.com.au). But note that high rents on The Esplanade mean high prices. Much better value (and food) can be found in the adjacent side streets.

Above: Palm Cove jetty
Left: crocodiles at Cairns Tropical Zoo

5. NORTHERN TABLELAND *(see map, p36)*

A day exploring the bush and agricultural land of the interior, covering a national park, the bush town of Mareeba and quaint Yungaburra village, with liqueurs, coffee and peanuts to taste along the way.

You may prefer a four-wheel-drive vehicle for this trip as there could be some driving over unsealed roads. Wherever you're staying, the Smithfield roundabout, 13km (8 miles) north of Cairns on the Captain Cook Highway, is your starting point for today. From here you'll take the Kennedy Highway towards Kuranda. If you want to link this with Itinerary 6 to make it an overnight trip, book accommodation in the Yungaburra area. Take swimming gear for a dip in the lake.

A few hundred metres after you turn off at the Smithfield roundabout, the road begins its 12-km (7½-mile) climb up the **Kuranda Range**. It's well made but winding (use second gear), and it requires the driver's full attention. The highway climbs through dense tropical rainforest, and 8km (5 miles) from the roundabout there's a scenic lookout on the right. A roadside sign alerts drivers to be on the lookout for crossing cassowaries. As the road reaches the top of the range, 660m (2,165ft) above sea level, there are glimpses of the rich rainforest.

Soon you'll cross the **Barron River bridge** and the outskirts of Kuranda. A few kilometres past the Kuranda turn-off you'll notice the vegetation suddenly changes from rainforest to dry sclerophyll forest or, as the Australians call it, 'dry bush'. The change is brought about by two factors – less rainfall and different soil. In this part of Queensland, the landscape is also characterised by the presence of large, bulbous termite mounds. This heralds the beginning of the **Cairns Highlands** – also referred to as the Atherton Tablelands – a rich, rolling territory that slopes upwards to the south, much of it cultivated for agriculture.

Davies Creek and Mareeba Town

After crossing Davies Creek, on the left is a road that leads to the **Davies Creek National Park**. The road is unsealed, so drive with caution. At 8km (5 miles) there's a series of small parking areas; the second one gives the best access to a stretch of the creek where it winds and falls through a granite gorge. If it's warm, take a quick dip in one of the dozens of rocky ponds in the area. Then head back onto the Kennedy Highway, where the bush soon gives way to open farmland with mango, citrus and avocado orchards. At Parramatta Creek, a turn-off leads to **Cairns Wildlife Safari Reserve** (tel: 07 4093 7777; www.cairnswildlifesafarireserve.com.au), where, if you wish, you can 'breakfast with the beasts'.

After the Davies Creek turn-off towards Mareeba, **Tichun Coffee Farm** (Tues–Sun 8.30am–4.30pm; tel: 07 4093 3092) has a good café featuring home-grown coffees, while about 5km (3 miles) further towards Mareeba, then 4½km (2.7 miles) to the right along Gilmore Road, **Jaques Coffee Plantation** (tel:

Right: north and west of the Cairns Highlands, the landscape becomes drier and dotted with termite mounds

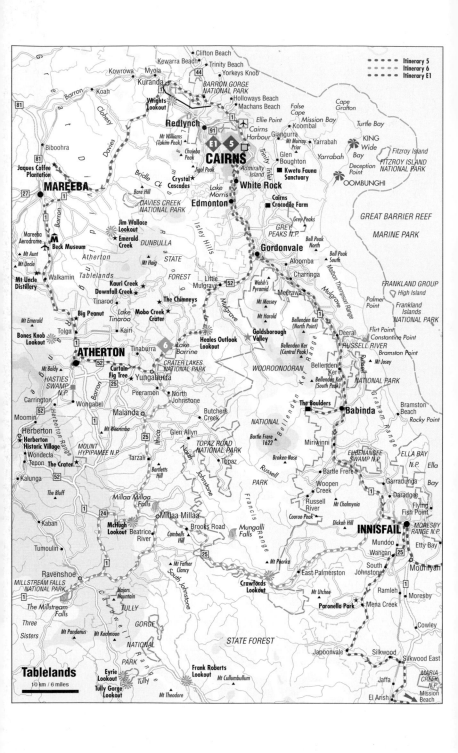

Itinerary 5
Itinerary 6
Itinerary E1

Clifton Beach
Kewarra Beach
Trinity Beach
Kowrowa
Myola
Yorkeys Knob
Kuranda
Wrights Lookout
Holloways Beach
Machans Beach
False Cape
Cape Grafton
Turtle Bay
Redlynch
Ellie Point
Mission Bay
Koombal
Mt Williams (Tokim Peak)
Chujeba Peak
Cairns Harbour
Giangurra
Mt Murray Prior
Yarrabah
KING Wide Bay
Fitzroy Island
CAIRNS
Jigol Peak
Glen Boughton
Yarrabah
Deception Point
FITZROY ISLAND NATIONAL PARK
Biboohra
Admiralty Island
Kwetu Fauna Sanctuary
OOMBUNGHI
Jaques Coffee Plantation
Crystal Cascades
White Rock
Bridle Ck
Bare Hill
Lake Morris
Edmonton
Cairns Crocodile Farm
GREAT BARRIER REEF
MAREEBA
DAVIES CREEK NATIONAL PARK
Grey Peaks
MARINE PARK
Jim Wallace Lookout
GREY PEAKS N.P.
Bell Peak North
Mareeba Aerodrome
Beck Museum
Emerald Creek
DUNBULLA
Gordonvale
Bell Peak South
Mt Aunt
Mt Uncle
Atherton
Aloomba
FRANKLAND GROUP
Mt Uncle Distillery
Walkamin
STATE
Mt Haig
Charringa
High Island
Tablelands
Kauri Creek
Little Mulgrave
Walsh's Pyramid
Merawa
Palmer Point
Frankland Islands NATIONAL PARK
Downfall Creek
FOREST
Tinaroo
The Chimneys
Mt Massey
Bellenden Ker (North Point)
Big Peanut
Lake Tinaroo
Mobo Creek Crater
Mt Harold
Deeral
RUSSELL RIVER
Constantine Point
Bones Knob Lookout
Kairi
Goldsborough Valley
Bellenden Ker (Central Peak)
Bramston Point
Tolga
Heales Outlook Lookout
Mt Josey
Lake Barrine
Bellenden Ker
ATHERTON
Tinaburra
CRATER LAKES NATIONAL PARK
WOOROONOORAN
Bellenden Ker (South Peak)
NATIONAL PARK
Mt Baldy
Curtain Fig Tree
Yungaburra
Graham Range
HASTIES SWAMP N.P.
Peeramon
The Boulders
Babinda
Bramston Beach
Carrington
Wongabel
North Johnstone
NATIONAL
Rocky Point
Moomin
Malanda
Butchers Creek
Bartle Frere 1622
Miriwinni
EUBENANGEE SWAMP N.P.
ELLA BAY N.P.
Herberton Historic Village
Mt Weerimba
Glen Allyn
Broken Nose
Ella Bay
Wondecla
Ithica
TOPAZ ROAD NATIONAL PARK
Bartle Frere
Garradunga
Tepon
The Crater
Tarzali
Topaz
Russell River
Woopen Creek
Daradgee
Kalunga
Bartletts Hill
Mt Chalmynia
Flying Fish Point
The Bluff
Millaa Millaa Falls
Russell River
Cooroo Peak
INNISFAIL
MORESBY RANGE N.P.
Kaban
Millaa Millaa
Brooks Road
Mungalli Falls
Dickah Hill
Mundoo
Etty Bay
McHugh Lookout
Beatrice River
Cambells Hill
Wangan
Tumoulin
Francis Range
South Johnstone
Mouriiyan
Ravenshoe
Mt Father Clancy
Mt Peorka
East Palmerston
MILLSTREAM FALLS NATIONAL PARK
Majors Mountain
Crawfords Lookout
Ramleh
Moresby
The Millstream Falls
Mt Utchee
Mena Creek
Three Sisters
Mt Pandanus
Mt Koolmoon
TULLY GORGE
Paronella Park
Cowley
STATE FOREST
NATIONAL
Japoonvale
Silkwood
Silkwood East

Tablelands
10 km / 6 miles

Eyrie Lookout
Tully Gorge Lookout
Frank Roberts Lookout
Mt Cullumbullum
Mt Theodore
Tully
Jaffa
El Arish
MARIA CREEK N.P.
Mission Beach

07 4093 3284), is home to the pioneers of coffee in northern Queensland. There are now 25,000 coffee bushes under cultivation and plans to plant another 60,000 by the end of 2009. You may even care to do a 20-minute wind-in-your-hair trial instructional flight in one of Jaques' microlight aircraft, for a super-scenic view of this rich agricultural area.

Back on the highway, proceed to the rural town of **Mareeba**, which, being inland from the Great Dividing Range, has 300 sunny days a year. The Mareeba district produces around 80 percent of Australia's coffee crop and the highlight of the local coffee scene is **The Coffee Works** (36 Mason Street, Mareeba; tel: 07 4092 4101), incorporating **Coffee World**, billed as having the world's largest collection of antique coffee-making implements and machinery. More than 2,000 items are on display, and the admission price of $19 includes unlimited tastings of 21 different coffees plus coffee liqueurs and a range of chocolates.

Historic Aircraft

Head south out of Mareeba on the Kennedy Highway. If you're into military memorabilia, you could spend an hour or more at two historic collections. The first, 5km (3 miles) south, is the **Beck Museum** (Sat–Sun 10am–3.30pm; admission charge; tel: 07 4092 3979), where enthusiast-owner Syd Beck is usually on hand to show you around. His extensive collection includes 1940s aircraft, vehicles and weaponry, most of it housed in a huge timber-framed hangar.

Almost opposite is Warbird Adventures at the **Mareeba Aerodrome**. The aerodrome was built in just eight days in March and April 1942 for USAF B17 Flying Fortresses, but was first occupied by the Royal Australian Air Force's

Above: take flight on Jaques' Plantation
Right: Beck Museum is for aircraft fans

100 Squadron, equipped with Beaufort torpedo bombers. A nostalgic flight in a vintage warbird is an option.

Continue southwards and when you reach Walkamin, turn right for a brief side-trip 2½km (1½ miles) along Hansen and Chewko roads to the **Mount Uncle Distillery** (daily 10am–5pm; tel: 07 4086 8008). The distillery dedicates itself to encapsulating fine locally grown products like coffee, honey, macadamia nuts, bananas, limes and mulberries into tongue-tingling liqueurs, and produces a memorable rum in the Queensland tradition. Bridges Tearoom and Café is also on-site.

About 18km (11 miles) further down the Kennedy Highway on the left is an important link to the region's World War II involvement. The **Rocky Creek Memorial Park** commemorates over 100,000 Allied servicemen and women who underwent tropical warfare training here during World War II. A plaque is displayed for each known unit.

Continue down the highway, and look out for the **Big Peanut** on the left as you enter **Tolga** township – hot, freshly roasted, locally grown peanuts can be sampled here. On the right just across the railway line, the **Tolga Woodworks Gallery and Café** (daily 9am–5pm; tel: 07 4095 4488) sells a stunning array of wooden furniture and ornaments – many of which are crafted on the premises.

Some 1½km (1 mile) south of town, the highway goes through **Tolga Scrub**, a luxuriant rainforest tract where native cedars and maples grow undisturbed ('tolga' is the Aboriginal word for 'big scrub').

Atherton and Yungaburra

There are other lunch alternatives at **Atherton**, a few minutes' drive south. Turn into Main Street, where two hotels offer an inexpensive lunch – the restored 1930s **Barron Valley Hotel** at 53 Main Street

Above: drinks at the Mount Uncle Distillery
Left: Tolga's Big Peanut – you can't miss it

(tel: 07 4091 1222) and the **Grand Hotel** (7 Vernon Street; tel: 07 4091 4899), an elegant old pub in North Queensland style. If you are interested in gemstones, call in at **The Crystal Cave** (69 Main Street; Mon–Fri 8.30am–5pm, Sat 8.30am–4pm, Sun 10am–4pm; admission charge; tel: 07 4091 2365; www.crystalcaves.com.au), where a fine display of natural crystals and fossils, including the world's largest amethyst geode, is set out in a simulated 'cave'.

From Atherton, follow the signs for Malanda and Herberton, then take a left turn where the signpost indicates that it's 12km (7½ miles) to Yungaburra. This is where you'll stay if you've elected to combine this and Itinerary 6 into a two-day trip *(see Accommodation, page 95)*.

Approaching Yungaburra, follow the sign to the **Curtain Fig Tree**. Walk along the boardwalk that surrounds the tree and an interpretive display explains how this amazing natural sculpture was formed. A draped curtain of aerial roots first grew from the parasitic fig, 'strangling' the host tree; the whole thing then fell sideways and the fig lowered its roots to the ground.

Continue into **Yungaburra**, the largest National Trust village in Queensland, with no fewer than 18 heritage-listed buildings. Have a stroll around, and, especially if you have children with you, go to the **Rainforest Gallery** (daily 8.30am–5pm; tel: 07 4095 2144), the only place where you can see the enchanting 'Rainforest Folk', fantasy creatures created by doll-maker Chris Boston. There is a wide range of quality crafts on sale here, more than 70 percent of them locally made.

Lake Eacham and Gordonvale

Spend the rest of the afternoon at **Lake Eacham**, a volcanic crater lake in the rainforest, off to the right about 3km (2 miles) along Gordonvale Road. You can swim in the placid water or follow the signposts to the Ranger Station to pick up leaflets on self-guided walks. There is a 3-km (2-mile) circuit around the lake, which is a cassowary habitat, and you're also likely to see scrub turkeys, pale-yellow robins and tooth-billed bower birds (found only in the Wet Tropics), and a range of water birds.

If returning to Cairns, it's 40km (25 miles) to Gordonvale through 17km (10½ miles) of lush World Heritage rainforest. For 19km (12 miles) it's a winding route, and there are two lookouts with great views over the valley below. From Gordonvale to Cairns, you'll cover 23km (14 miles) of the Bruce Highway, an easy but sometimes busy road.

If staying overnight, return to Yungaburra, where the top spot for dinner (equally good for lunch) is **Nick's Swiss-Italian Restaurant** (33 Gillies Highway; lunch Fri–Sun, dinner Tues–Sun; reservations required; tel: 07 4095 3330). Lots of Nick's personal energy goes into your entertainment; often, when priorities allow it, he whips out his accordion to help you enjoy your selected dish – a memorable example of which is grilled lamb loin with brandy garlic butter.

Right: chef Nick also entertains at his restaurant in Yungaburra

6. SOUTHERN TABLELAND *(see map, p36)*

Cruise through the rainforest, then explore pastoral landscapes before visiting some spectacular waterfalls.

This itinerary can be done on its own or as an extension of Itinerary 5 (see pages 35–9). Get to Lake Barrine National Park in time to have breakfast at the Tea House Restaurant and be ready for the first sailing of the Lake Barrine Rainforest Cruise at 10.15am – it's an hour from Cairns, two hours from Port Douglas, 10 minutes from Yungaburra. From points north of Cairns go south on the Captain Cook Highway, then from Cairns continue further south on the Bruce Highway for about 23km (14 miles). Just beyond Gordonvale, turn right onto the Gillies Highway and, in about 34km (21 miles), Lake Barrine is off to the left. If you stayed the night in Yungaburra (see page 39), take the Gillies Highway east for about 9km (5½ miles) and Lake Barrine will be on the right. Bring swimming gear for a dip in a waterfall pool.

Have breakfast at the **Tea House Restaurant** (daily 9am–5pm; tel: 07 4095 3847). While you're waiting for the **Lake Barrine Rainforest Cruise** (details same as restaurant), take a look at the informative display on the forces that shaped this large volcanic crater lake. Take particular note of the plant specimen ('Gympie-Gympie') in a glass case – it's a stinging plant that you will want to avoid. You'll spend nearly an hour on this fascinating cruise around the perimeter of the lake, with an informative wildlife commentary.

The trip is equally interesting even if it rains, and in the cooler months you're likely to see amethystine pythons, the world's third largest snake (up to 8.5m/28ft long) sunning themselves on branches. Pelicans and other water birds are usually prolific, and you'll see eels, tortoises and fish in the calm waters. You'll be on the road by 11.30am, unless you decide to walk the 6-km (4-mile) Lake Barrine circuit path (which will take two hours more). A shorter 150-m (500-ft) walk from the Teahouse will take you to the giant twin Kauri pines, estimated to be 1,000 years old.

Tablelands Villages and Pastures

Back on the Gillies Highway, go west and continue through the Tablelands villages of Malanda and Tarzali, amid lush green hillside pastures with fertile red volcanic soil. The black and white Friesian cows grazing in these pastures each produce up to 30 litres (6½ gallons) of milk a day. The **Malanda Dairy Centre** runs informative tours (Tues–Thur 9am–3pm; admission charge;

bookings recommended; tel: 07 4095 1234). Another local attraction is the Nerada Tea Plantation (Australia's largest) in Glen Allyn Road, Malanda (daily 9am–4pm; tel: 07 4096 8328).

Go through Tarzali and after 7km (4¼ miles), turn right onto Ravenshoe Road, and follow signs to the **McHugh Lookout**, from where you have sweeping views over the tablelands towards Queensland's two highest mountains – **Mount Bellenden Ker** at 1,593m (5,225ft) and the 1,622-m (5,322-ft) **Mount Bartle Frere**. Continue to a T-junction, about 10 minutes' drive further on, and turn left onto the Kennedy Highway, following the signs to Ravenshoe (pronounced 'raven's hoe').

After you've passed through a magnificent natural avenue of tall, elegant white Rose Gums with the apt botanical title of *Eucalyptus grandis*, the **Windy Hill Wind Farm** is sure to catch your eye, with the giant 22-m (72-ft) long blades of 20 graceful three-bladed windmills swishing musically in the breeze. Each tower stands about 43m (140ft) high, and they generate enough electricity to supply about 3,500 homes, preventing the possible release into the atmosphere of 25,000 tonnes of carbon dioxide that are produced by conventional methods of power generation per year.

Between Atherton and Ravenshoe, **Herberton Historic Village** (6 Broadway, Herberton; tel: 07 4096 2002; www.herbertonhistoricvillage.com.au) is an authentic re-creation of Herberton as it was in the 1870s – everything from a pub to a live-in bank, shops, a schoolhouse and a 1929 rail ambulance.

High-Altitude Ravenshoe

In another 5km (3 miles), you'll reach **Ravenshoe**, set up in the 1880s at the top of the Great Dividing Range, 920m (3,000ft) above sea level, as a centre for the timber and agriculture industries. At the **Ravenshoe Visitor Centre** (24 Moore Street; tel: 07 4097 7700), on the right as you enter town, pick up a leaflet on the windmills, and a map with a list of nearby waterfalls in tropical surroundings; try and visit at least one of them.

The centre houses the Nganyaji Interpretive Centre, showcasing the culture of the region's Jirrbal people, whose language is the oldest one spoken in the world.

Left: Lake Barrine's Teahouse Restaurant. **Above:** cows at a pasture near Malanda. **Right:** signage at Ravenshoe

If you are hungry, lunch alfresco at the **Popular Café** (tel: 07 4097 7373) at 66 Grigg Street. After lunch check out some of 'Queensland's highests': the **Hotel Tully Falls** reckons it's the highest hotel; there's also the highest bakery; and at the top of the street is the highest pub. Opposite the pub, the attractive **Win's Gallery** relies not on altitude but on solitude, depicted atmospherically by artist-in-residence, Winsome Broad.

Gorges and Waterfalls

Some 5km (3 miles) out of town, at the end of an unsealed road off the Mount Garnet Road, is **Millstream Falls**; while **Little Millstream Falls** is 2km (1¼ miles) on another (sealed) road, and is actually not so little. A steep five-minute walk down into the gorge is rewarded by memorable tropical scenery. In this sheltered chasm the mist and vapour from the waterfalls provides a permanent greenhouse atmosphere.

Return to a sign on the right saying 'Millaa Millaa 29km' and follow the road for 2½km (1½ miles) until another sign directs you to the 'Scenic Route' (24km/15 miles to Millaa Millaa), a narrow road that winds through lovely farmland and virgin rainforest. Just beyond the township turn left to **Millaa Millaa Falls**, probably the most photographed of the lot.

If you need a snack, stop at the **Falls Teahouse** (Fri–Wed 10am–5pm) at the turn-off. Just off the road, the falls descend rather noisily into a large pool. There are parking facilities, toilets and changing rooms, and you can swim across to the waterfall, sit on the rocks and let the cold, falling water pummel you.

Above: picturesque Millaa Millaa Falls
Left: explore trails and creeks near Millaa Millaa

Homeward Bound

Homeward bound, take the Palmerston Highway towards Innisfail, then in 5km (3 miles) turn left near the 'steep descent' sign, where there's a Brooks Road sign on the left. This short rural loop road takes you through the hills and valleys past the **Mungalli Creek Dairy**, with its 'Farmhouse Cheesery' and the **Mungalli Falls Tourist Centre** (daily 9am–5pm; tel: 07 4097 2358; www.mungallifalls.com). Horse riding is available by appointment, there are some picturesque swimming pools in the creek, and if you're staying longer in the area, there are also nocturnal glow-worm tours.

You'll come back to the sweeping Palmerston Highway, which descends through 14km (8 miles) of lush rainforest. Along the way are signs to several attractive rest areas, some with walking trails to even more waterfalls, and a campsite at **Henrietta Creek**. At **Crawford's Lookout** there are views through a clearing down to the North Johnstone River, where you may see white-water rafters. Also here is one of the region's top new attractions, the 1,400-m (4,600-ft) **Mamu Rainforest Canopy Walkway** (daily 9.30am–5.30pm; tel: 07 4064 5294). The walkway, with a cantilever and observation tower, provides spectacular views of the World Heritage listed rainforest.

Further along, the road descends until you see a huge banana plantation on the left and the **Nucifora Tea Plantation** on the right. Watch out for sugar cane trains during the harvest season. Approaching Innisfail, you reach a junction where there is an avenue of stately Royal Palms. Turn left onto Bruce Highway and the 1¼-hour drive to Cairns is on 84km (52 miles) of mostly excellent road.

7. CAPE TRIBULATION *(see map, p44)*

Go crocodile-spotting on a river cruise, spend time in the rainforest at the excellent Environmental Centre, then take a quick beach break before heading out to Cape Tribulation.

Your starting time today is set by the need to be at the Daintree River by 9.15am for a 9.30am departure – it's 1¼ hours from Cairns; 40 minutes from Port Douglas. Book ahead for either of the one-hour river cruises (River Train, tel: 07 4090 7676; Bruce Belcher's, tel: 07 4098 7717). There's scope for a little mixing and matching in this itinerary, in case you want to stay longer at one attraction and forego another; or even stay overnight in the Cape Tribulation area. Bring swimming gear and binoculars.

If you're based anywhere between Cairns and Palm Cove, make sure that you set out early enough (6.30am from Cairns) to allow time for breakfast-with-a-view at the **Ellis Beach Bar and Grill** (daily 6.30am–8pm or later; tel: 07 4055 3534), about 30km (18 miles) north of Cairns on the left.

Above: fresh fruit from a roadside stall, Palmerston Highway

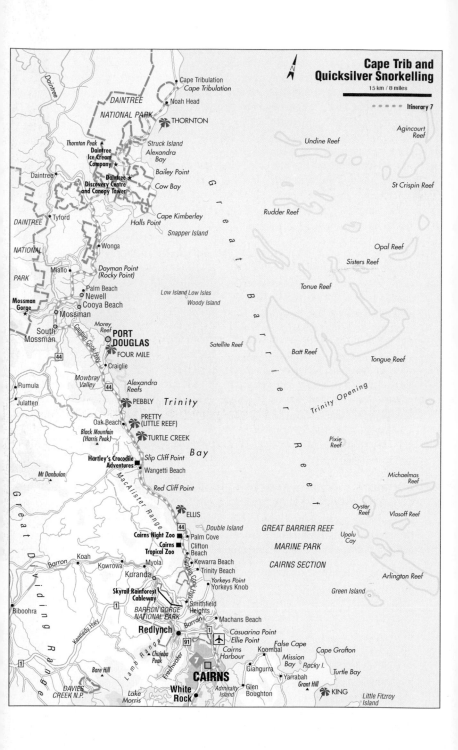

**Cape Trib and
Quicksilver Snorkelling**

15 km / 8 miles

●●●●● Itinerary 7

Go north on Captain Cook Highway, and 10km (6 miles) beyond the turnoff to Port Douglas you'll reach **Mossman** *(see Itinerary 2, page 26).* Drive through the small town, heading for the Daintree River ferry crossing. At the Miallo Y-junction, take the right fork, which leads to the ferry crossing. If you're booked on the **River Train** (tel: 07 4090 7676; www.daintreerivertrain.com), a quaint string of small 'carriages' that snakes its way through even the narrowest reaches of the river, follow the signage: the left lane is for the ferry, and the right takes you to the River Train car park.

The other operator is **Bruce Belcher's Daintree River Cruises** (daily 9.30am–4pm; tel: 07 4098 7717; www.daintreerivercruises.com.au), a more conventional craft with equally good views for crocodile spotting (binoculars provided), 3km (2 miles) beyond the ferry turn-off on the road to Daintree Village. Both operators give excellent commentaries on the river's ecosystems and wildlife.

The tours take you up- or downstream, depending on weather and tide factors, through narrow reaches lined with mangroves or rainforests that are rich in wildlife. It's unusual not to spot a crocodile (from a safe distance) especially in the cooler months when the huge reptiles come out of the water to sun themselves on the river banks. When crocodiles are spotted, the boat's motors are shut down for a while and you drift in peaceful silence.

Daintree Discovery Centre

By about 10.45am you're back and on board the car ferry for the brief river crossing. On the other side is a good sealed road (watch out for cassowaries, large flightless birds which pose a hazard for motorists as they suddenly dash across the road) and you'll be headed north again, through rainforest and farmland. After 8km (5 miles)

Above: family of cyclists heading for Daintree
Right: view from Alexandra Range Lookout

you'll be at the **Alexandra Range Lookout**, with sweeping views back to the south, across the wide mouth of the Daintree River, Snapper Island and the sugar cane fields and ranges beyond. The road beyond here is well made but narrow and winding, and it requires the driver's full attention.

Some 2km (1¼ miles) from the lookout turn right into Tulip Oak Road for the **Daintree Discovery Centre** (daily 8.30am–5pm; tel: 07 4098 9171; www.daintree-rec.com.au), a world-class interpretive centre that is privately owned, but affiliated to the Wet Tropics Management Authority. It provides a self-guided rainforest booklet and ample interpretive material, including a display centre and theatre (admission charge), all giving an excellent insight into what you will see here, from the low-impact boardwalk and the breathtaking heights of the tree-top **Canopy Tower**. At 23m (76ft) high, and with five large viewing platforms at different levels, the tower provides a marvellous experience for photographers, botany enthusiasts and bird watchers – and you can almost feel the trees around you exuding oxygen.

There are also audio guided tours in several languages and a 'bush tucker trail'. Many visitors spend hours here, and, because it offers far more than a quick rainforest fix, you can have your booklet stamped for a repeat visit within seven days.

A Break at the Beach

A little further on is a sign on the left for the **Daintree Ice Cream Company** (daily 11am–5pm; tel:

Above: a close-up of the rainforest
Left: Coconut Beach Resort

07 4098 9114), which produces ice cream flavoured with locally grown tropical fruits, according to season. They are all worth savouring – coconut, mango, wattleseed, jackfruit and black sapote. If it's too close to lunchtime, you can return here on your way back later in the day.

The road remains inland, winding through rich rainforest and farmland until you reach **Thornton Beach**, where there is ample space for parking and a beautiful uncrowded tract of beach if you fancy a quick swim or a laze in the sun. Continue along the next 8km (5 miles) of winding road, which has some truly brutal speed bumps to slow you down, then on the right you'll see the car park for the **Cape Tribulation Resort and Spa** (tel: 07 4098 0033; www.capetribulation.com.au), which is recommended for lunch (daily 12.30–2pm). There's a boardwalk over the pandanus swamp to the elegant timber **Cape Restaurant and Bar**, right on the beach, where the bar and stools are made from large chunks of rainforest timbers. You can sit by the pool or inside, and choose from the à la carte menu. Lunch guests can use the pool, or walk down to the beach.

To the Cape

When you've had enough lazing around, you haven't far to go. Less than 1km (½ mile) up the road the sign reads **Cape Tribulation North**, the northern side of the Cape, which protrudes at right angles from the main coastline. You will also see 'Kulki' on the signs, which is the traditional aboriginal name for this visitor magnet. Turn right here into the parking area (with picnic tables and toilets), which has a 400-m (¼-mile) boardwalk to an elevated viewing platform. It can be congested here, so if you are not determined to see the actual headland, you might want to stay on at nearby Coconut Beach instead.

From the parking area there's a short signposted walk over the saddle west of the headland to **Myall Beach**. Don't be alarmed by the goannas (large lizards) which hang out here scavenging the crumbs from the picnickers' tables. The Cape is not without its hostile inhabitants: the beaches have signs warning of stinging box jellyfish, which are prevalent from October to May (vinegar is provided near beach entrances for quick treatment), and you are advised not to swim in or near river estuaries, home of saltwater crocodiles; even cassowaries can attack, though it's more likely that they'll avoid you.

From here on, the road is unsealed and suitable only for high-clearance four-wheel-drive vehicles, so returning the way you came is the only option. **Mount Sorrow** and **Thornton's Peak** loom on the right, their peaks often shrouded in mist. The drive back to Cairns will take about two hours (and traffic can be heavy). Between Miallo and Mossman, detour right into Scomazzon Road for **Scomazzons Roadside Stall**, where you can buy locally grown fruit, including, pineapples, strawberry papaw (papaya) and custard apples.

MARINE STINGERS ARE PRESENT IN THESE WATERS DURING THE SUMMER MONTHS

Right: be careful where you swim in the summer

8. QUICKSILVER SNORKELLING *(see map, p44)*

A fun day trip to the outer Great Barrier Reef, with diving and snorkelling tuition for first-timers, and dry exploring in a semi-submersible boat for non-swimmers.

Several operators do such trips (see page 74) but Port Douglas-based Quicksilver, the most expensive outfit, is also the best. Call Quicksilver in advance (tel: 07 4087 2100; www.quicksilver-cruises.com) to book the trip. You can arrange a coach pick-up when you book, and you have the option of joining the vessel at Cairns' Reef Fleet Terminal (departs 8am), Palm Cove Jetty (departs 8.35am) or Port Douglas (departs 10am). Prices start from AU$197 per person, but note that Introductory Dives are an optional extra. Bring swimming gear and sun protection. There's also a purpose-designed chair-lift to help wheelchair-bound visitors into the water.

Winner of many tourism awards, Quicksilver is well known for its attention to safety and friendliness. Its *Wavepiercer* is a high-speed Cairns-built catamaran with a shallow draft that is eminently suitable for reef operations. Its specially designed hulls literally pierce the waves to eliminate pitching. If you boarded the *Wavepiercer* from either Cairns or Palm Cove, sit back and enjoy the coastal scenery to Port Douglas. After the final pick-up of passengers at Port Douglas, you head for the outer reef. While underway, visit the bow and watch the wavepiercing action of the hulls, sometimes with fun-loving dolphins matching the catamaran's speed.

Before arrival at the huge two-storey floating pontoon, 39 nautical miles offshore, you will be briefed on its many attrac–

Above: snorkellers at Agincourt Reef
Left: creative sun protection

tions and how best to enjoy them. Quicksilver's deep commitment to environmental responsibility becomes readily apparent – the company employs 10 marine biologists. **Agincourt Reef**, where you are heading, is particularly rich in marine life because it's right at the edge of Australia's continental shelf. Beyond it the seabed drops away to a depth of 500m (1,640ft), so the waters lapping the reef have different characteristics from those on the landward side.

Many are content to just snorkel, but even if you have no previous underwater experience, you can have an 'escorted dive' with an instructor literally holding your hand. It's not a dive course and you won't get a certificate, but it can count towards Quicksilver's full four- or five-day courses, for which you may be inspired to enrol. In the forward cabin you're given a thorough half-hour briefing on the use of the equipment, emergency signals and what to expect, followed by 10 to 20 minutes' familiarisation with the equipment.

Exploring Agincourt Reef

On arrival in the Agincourt Reef area, each instructor takes four people and for 30 to 40 minutes shows them the magnificent creatures of the reef – the fish, corals and giant clams – and you can buy a video of your first underwater adventure. Freshwater showers and changing rooms are provided on the pontoon. Taking the escorted dive will still allow plenty of time to enjoy the rest of the reef experience. Snorkels and masks are provided, along with

instruction in their use. The staff will help you get accustomed to breathing underwater before setting out amongst the coral 'bommies' – isolated coral outcrops reaching up from the sandy bottom, which attract hosts of colourful fish. All snorkelling is done in a roped area and supervised by safety staff. Fish feeding, between noon and 1.10pm, attracts a regular following from the deep, and optional extras include 'adventure snorkelling' at a more remote site, in a small group accompanied by a marine biologist.

If you don't want to get into the water, there's plenty to enjoy, including an underwater viewing area from which you can watch the divers, and a semi-submersible in which you can tour the coral without getting wet. For an extra charge, you can have a brief helicopter flight over the reef or arrange a scenic helicopter flight back to Port Douglas or Cairns.

If you remain aboard the *Wavepiercer* for the trip home, a well-stocked bar is available to conclude your enjoyable day. Whichever way you decide to return to dry land, at 2.40pm, a blast on the ship's horn is the signal for you to return to the pontoon in preparation for departure.

Right: the *Wavepiercer* docked at its pontoon at Agincourt Reef

Excursions

1. MISSION BEACH AND DUNK ISLAND
(see map p36 and p52)

A two-day journey (or longer, depending on whether you extend your stay at Mission Beach or Dunk Island). Head south to see a rainforest World Heritage Site, a Spanish-style castle and a luxuriant tropical island, with bush walking, swimming, sailing and snorkelling.

Book ahead for accommodation at the Dunk Island Resort (tel: 07 4068 8199; www.voyages.com.au); also book for the 4.30pm Water Taxi (tel: 07 4068 8310) to Dunk Island and for the Quick Cat Cruise (tel: 07 4068 7289) if you plan to take up that option. Wherever you're based, you need to set out early – 7.30am from Cairns; earlier if you are further north. First, make your way to Cairns, then take the Bruce Highway south and follow directions below. Take what you need for an overnight stay, including sturdy walking shoes, swimming gear and sun protection. Depending on the time of year, you might need an umbrella.

Travelling south on the Bruce Highway, you'll pass through Edmonton and Gordonvale; then 23km (14¼ miles) from Cairns, if it's crushing season, you'll see the white plume of smoke from the Mulgrave Sugar Mill. Straight ahead is the aptly-named **Walsh's Pyramid**, a forbidding 922-m (3,025-ft) monolith where the annual 'mountain man race' is held – usually the winner scales it in less than 1½ hours, but 2½ is more realistic if you're tempted to enter.

Rainfall and Rainforest

As you pass through the sugar cane fields, notice the increasing richness of the tropical greenery. You're approaching the Australian mainland's area of highest rainfall, measured not in millimetres but in metres! **Babinda** and nearby **Tully** compete annually for the 'Golden Gumboot Award', which goes to the town recording the highest annual average: usually around 4.6m (over 15ft). The locals (who, even with this record, still tend to exaggerate) will tell you it rains for 11 months, and drips off the trees for the rest of the year. In fact, large amounts of rain tend to fall in a very short time, and there's plenty of tropical sunshine to add its influence to the unusually diverse vegetation.

At Babinda, just after you pass the historic sugar mill, turn right and follow signs to **The Boulders**, a Wet Tropics World Heritage area with a nature reserve and visitor facilities (toilets, picnic tables, well-marked trails). The 850-m (½-mile) **Rainforest Circuit** walk takes you across a suspension bridge and to clear pools where you can cool off amidst massed green foliage, giant tree ferns, moss covered boulders, coiled and curling vines and tall, ancient trees. A

Left: Mission Beach
Right: intrepid young explorer

second, shorter walk leads to the **Boulders Gorge** past the Devils Pool. The stream rises in the high country between Queensland's two tallest mountains, where rainfall of 600mm (nearly 2ft) has been recorded in a 24-hour period.

Don't even think about swimming here because there have been a number of drownings, especially of young men who have slipped on the rocks and been trapped under the surging cascades. Legend has it that they are lured by the singing of the spirit of Oolana, a beautiful young Aboriginal woman, betrothed to a respected elder, who fell in love with a visitor from a neighbouring tribe. They ran away, but were found here by the water's edge, and as Oolana's tribe dragged her back she broke away and flung herself into the gentle waters of the creek. Just then a tremendous upheaval occurred – the land shook with sorrow, and rushing water came cascading over the whole area. Huge boulders were thrown up and she disappeared among them. They say that her spirit remains and her anguished cry can sometimes be heard, calling her lover to return.

The Spaniard's Castle

Back in **Babinda**, call in at **Babinda and District Arts and Crafts Co-op** (15 Munro Street; daily 9am–4pm; tel: 07 4067 2044). Staffed by volunteers, it stocks a diversity of craftwork, including wooden bowls of hand-crafted 'fruits of the tropical rainforest' – a bright display ranging from the blue quandong fruit to the glossy red fruit of the lacewing vine, perfect replicas of the colourful flashes you may see in the rainforest.

Head south again on the Bruce Highway. The drive to **Innisfail** is a scenic one, with jungle-clad mountains fringing rich farmland. Drive through Innisfail and go straight ahead to **South Johnstone**, with the South Johnstone River on your left – do not swim here, it's the home of the usually hungry *Crocodylus Johnstoni*, which grows to about 5m (16½ ft). Keeping a lookout for sugar cane trains in season, drive through the banana, papaw, citrus and sugar cane farms to **Paronella Park** (daily 9am–7.30pm; admission charge; tel: 07 4065 3225; www.paronellapark. com.au). Here, the partially

Above: scenic Boulders Gorge

Map: Mission Beach and Dunk Island

5 km / 3 miles

- - - - Itinerary E1

MARIA CREEK NATIONAL PARK
Cassowary Coast
E1
Cairns
CLUMP MOUNTAIN NATIONAL PARK
South Maria Ck
Garners Point
Ninney Point
Bingil Bay
Bicton Hill
★ Lacey Creek
Clump Point
Mission Beach
GREAT BARRIER REEF MARINE PARK
Luff Hill
✿ MISSION
Wongaling Beach
Mt Tim O'Shanter
Tully
Purtaboi Island
Toogan Toogan Pt
Pall-Koo-Loo Pt
★ Dunk Island Resort
Dunk Island
Beaver Cay Reef
Lugger Bay
Coconut Bay
HULL RIVER NATIONAL PARK
Tam O'Shanter Point

restored ruins of North Queensland's first tourist attraction lie in 5ha (13 acres) of rainforest. It was built by José Paronella, a young Spanish immigrant who fell in love with the region in 1913 and eventually purchased the property and built a home there. He then went on to construct a down-scaled Spanish castle beside the **Mena Creek Falls** and surround it with pleasure gardens, which was designed for public enjoyment. If the old castle does not interest you, an alternative is to continue down the Bruce Highway from Innisfail to Mourilyan, make a brief side-trip to **Etty Bay** and picnic at one of the prettiest beaches on the whole coastline.

From the castle, you are about 45 minutes from **Mission Beach**. Follow the signs through even greener rural land to Silkwood (23km/14 miles), and in 3km (2 miles) turn right onto the highway and continue to El Arish. Turn left, and 16km (10 miles) of sometimes winding road takes you to the Mission Beach area – five communities strung out along a coastline of broad white-sand beaches backed by coconut palms and lapped by (usually) crystal-blue water.

You should have some time to spare before your pre-booked place on the 4.30pm water taxi to Dunk Island, so call in at **Mission Beach Tourism** (daily 9am–5pm; tel: 07 4068 7099; www.missionbeachtourism.com) for information, then go next door to the **Environment Centre** (daily 10am–4pm) to watch a 10-minute video on the rare and endangered cassowary, which still exists in notable numbers in the rainforests. If you decide to extend your stay at the Mission Beach area, there is an ample range of hotels to meet all budgets *(see page 96)*.

Dunk Island

Take the South Mission Beach Road to the **Water Taxi** (tel: 07 4068 8310) departure point in **Banfield Parade** on Wongaling Beach. Park your car in the open paddock at the rear of the office; note that you'll be wading out through shallow (warm) water to board the boat – anything below your knees will be getting wet (staff will load your baggage). In 15 minutes you'll be on the jetty at **Dunk Island**, where a resort bus will be waiting to take you to the reception desk to check in. Dunk Island is the self-styled 'Island of Peace and Plenty', a translation of its Aboriginal name, 'Coonanglebah', and the accommodation options range from standard twin-bedded rooms to suites and cabanas.

As the sun sets over the mainland mountains, tiny candles light the stairways and tables and the tropical night comes alive. Try a pre-dinner 'E J Banfield' cocktail, named after the first white settler who famously heard 'the beat of a different drum' and stayed on the island for 25 years, eventually writing his well-known book, *Confessions of a Beachcomber*. You can dine from a bounteous beachside barbecue or à la carte, and there will probably be live entertainment. Dunk Island is particularly good for families, with a

Right: Japanese tourists at the suspension bridge over Mena Creek Falls, Paronella Park

babysitting service, child-care provided by the Kids' Club and a teenage club for those up to 16 years, offering all kinds of fun. There are plenty of activities included in the price of your accommodation, and you might want to stay for more than one night to take full advantage of them. The resort also provides maps of the bushwalking tracks and lists of the interesting birdlife you might be able to identify along the way.

You should also set aside some time to walk (40 minutes) to **Bruce Arthur's Artists' Colony** (Mon and Thur only 10am–1pm), an enclave of distinguished artists-in-residence exhibiting Dunk Island-produced paint-

ings, pottery and jewellery. If you're tempted to purchase something from the display, it will be packed and delivered to your room at the resort. You can then return the way you came, or complete a rainforest circuit track, which will take you about another 1½ hours, with some stunning views of the island-studded bay.

Beaver Cay

Among the options at Dunk Island resort is a cruise with **Quick Cat Cruises** (departure 10.45am; tel: 07 4068 7289; www.quickcatcruises.com.au; reservations required) to **Beaver Cay** reef, 25 nautical miles off the coast. If you're returning to the mainland later on the same day, check out by 11am before you set off on the cruise, and make arrangements for your baggage to be put aboard the vessel when it calls back at Dunk Island after the reef trip. A buffet lunch is served on board, after which you can spend your day diving, if you're a certified diver, or snorkelling – solo if you're experienced, with a guide if you're not. You can also do an 'introductory dive' under the guidance of a qualified instructor.

The voyage includes a trip in a glass-bottomed boat – the large spangled emperor fish underwater make you wonder who's watching whom – and snorkelling equipment is available on board. Beaver Cay has no vegetation, just a few migratory birds walking the soft, pale golden sand. Like a true desert island it's very exposed on a hot day, so put on plenty of sunscreen. Whales are sometimes sighted here during the migratory months of July and August.

The Quick Cat leaves Beaver Cay at about 3.15pm, stopping to pick up passengers who opted out of the cruise (and your luggage) at Dunk at 4.30pm, arriving on the mainland at **Clump Point** by 5pm. A courtesy bus will drop you back at your car (or hotel, if you are staying on in the Mission Beach area). Then you simply backtrack to the Bruce Highway and head north – it's about two hours to Cairns and three hours to Port Douglas.

Above: diving into Beaver Cay
Right: Dunk Island

2. CRUISING THE CORAL COAST *(see map, p56)*

A four-night cruise that follows the course of Captain Cook's voyage, calling at Fitzroy Island and Cooktown, before heading out to the coral cays and islands of the Great Barrier Reef.

Book well in advance with Captain Cook Cruises (tel: 02 9208 1100, toll-free 1800 221 080 or 1800 804 043; www.captaincook.com.au). Berths are frequently sold out, especially during high season. The price (starting at under AU$1,650 at time of press) includes all meals, entertainment and activities. You'll need to bring swimwear and suitable clothing for trips ashore, walking shoes and sun-protection, a camera (preferably with a polarising filter) and binoculars, if you have them. If you want to dive bring your Open Water Dive Certificate. You'll need to be at Cairns by 1pm, for departure at 2pm on Monday; you'll arrive back at 8am on Friday.

The MV *Reef Endeavour*, because it is especially designed and equipped for reef cruising, offers rare insights into some of the more remote and unspoiled parts of the Great Barrier Reef. There is also a three-night cruise to the south, but I recommend the northern circuit because it takes you to some locations that are hard to reach any other way. Accommodation is either in staterooms that open onto the outside deck, or cabins that open onto inside passageways (with portholes giving good natural lighting); some have double beds, but most have twin beds and all have en suite bathrooms.

On-board facilities include a swimming pool, sauna, spa and gym, and the relatively small passenger complement (about 150) makes for a friendly atmosphere. Daily information bulletins keep you posted on the ship's itinerary and activities, and safety is carefully observed – everyone is counted off and back on to the vessel at every stop.

Above: the MV *Reef Endeavour* is perfect for exploring the Great Barrier Reef

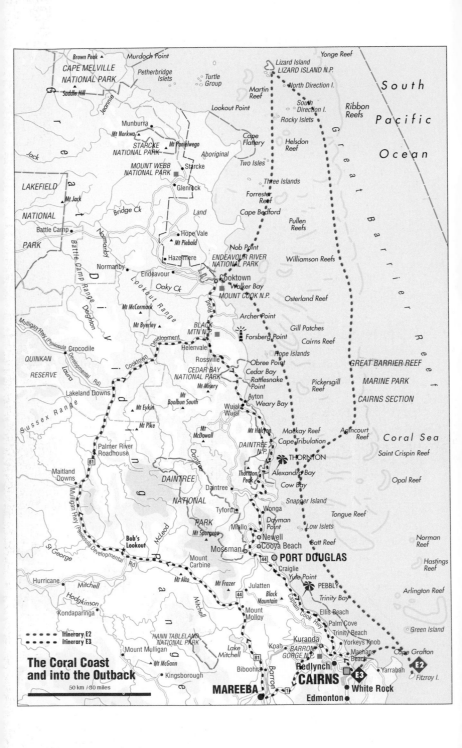

Day One – Monday

The first afternoon sees you sailing northeast down Trinity Inlet, past the granite faces of False Cape and Cape Grafton, to anchor off **Fitzroy Island** by 4pm. This rainforested mountain juts from the sea, much of it fringed by coral, and you are taken ashore on shuttle boats (try to get on the first one). You're ashore for two hours, with plenty of time (weather permitting) for a hike to the lighthouse, atop the island's highest peak. The 1½-hour walk is reasonably easy and well-marked, and takes you through tracts of magnificent rainforest with glimpses of the sea. If you're staying on the beach, you still need to wear shoes because it's not sand, but crushed coral. The last boat returns to the ship at 6pm, in time for dinner at 7.30. Dinners on board are à la carte; breakfasts and lunches are buffet style with plenty of choice and an emphasis on tropical fruit and regional produce.

As your voyage unfolds you can follow your progress in the Chart House Lounge, right at the top of the ship. Much of the first night's voyage closely resembles the route followed by Captain James Cook, who first discovered and charted most of Australia's east coast *(see page 11)*. The charts will show you the hundreds of reefs and shoals dotted between the mainland and the outer Barrier Reef. Cook was an extremely precise navigator, but without charts he had to rely on a masthead lookout. Tonight, guided by detailed charts, beacons and satellite navigation, you'll be passing close to the point where, for Cook, that lookout was not enough.

Day Two – Tuesday

Your Tuesday itinerary starts with a trip ashore to visit **Cooktown** *(see also page 61)* where an optional commentated minibus tour (for a small additional fee) ensures you'll take in as much as possible on this brief visit. If you don't avail yourself of the bus tour, head straight for the **James Cook Historical Museum** *(see page 61)*, which encapsulates most of the town's colourful history. Cook spent 48 days here, but you'll be back aboard at about 11.30am, again closely following his route northwards.

The next stop is at **Two Isles**, the only true coral cay on your itinerary, where you can snorkel and/or take the rewarding 45-minute beach walk right around the island in the company of an experienced biologist. You'll then pass a number of typical coral cays, more numerous in this area than almost anywhere else along the Great Barrier Reef, which are characterised by the low elevation of their richly vegetated sand dunes, the vivid white coral sand of their beaches, and the opalescent colour that the underlying coral imparts to the shallow blue water inside their fringing reefs.

Sailing on, you'll see ahead the towering granite bulk of **Lizard Island** (named by Cook), with its **Blue Lagoon** – a large expanse

Right: sundeck, MV Reef *Endeavour*

of coral-studded shallows inside a fringing reef that joins Lizard with two other islands. Around dusk, you drop anchor in **Watson's Bay**, in the lee of the island, named after an early settler, Mary Watson, who, along with her baby and two Chinese servants, perished at sea while fleeing from marauding mainland Aboriginal tribes. Just around the headland is luxurious **Lizard Island Lodge**, a playground for the rich and famous; non-residents are discouraged.

Day Three – Wednesday

The first (optional) attraction is only a good idea if you are fairly fit. Book an early call, put on some durable walking footwear and join a guided pre-breakfast walk up the rocky spine of Lizard Island to **Cook's Look**, at 359m (1,179ft) the island's highest point. Frustrated by what he described as a 'labyrinth' of coral shoals, Cook ascended this same hill in his quest for a way to open water. He saw the white lines of breakers, similar to those that you will observe crashing onto the reefs, and identified a safe passage through. There are two guides on your walk – a leader and another to take care of anybody who may find the pace too rapid. If that includes you, you will take a break at a spot with great views, amid the diverse native vegetation (including orchids and flowering trees), and wait until the others return. Back on the beach, you're ferried to the ship for a well-earned breakfast.

For the rest of the day, the ship provides shuttles to and from the beach, where you can snorkel in the clear water in a marked-out and patrolled area, enjoy the coral from a glass-bottomed boat, or sunbathe (taking care to protect yourself in this exposed environment). The crew set up a base camp with cool drinks, fresh towels and spare snorkelling equipment. After lunch on the ship, there's a guided walk of about 5km (3 miles) along a relatively flat path to the Blue Lagoon, where you can enjoy the solitude of its lovely beaches and swim in its calm waters. There is, however, no snorkelling here. You return, as usual, to the ship for dinner and evening entertainment.

Day Four – Thursday

Your overnight voyage will have brought you to the **Ribbon Reefs**, where the edge of the Great Barrier Reef is most clearly defined and the deep blue

water beyond attracts the giant black marlin, which millionaire sailors pursue relentlessly (but not always successfully). Ahead are the aqua-coloured shallows of the reef at its best, and across the lagoon you'll clearly see the line of surf beating incessantly on the reef's seaward side. The day is filled with options for diving, snorkelling or viewing from a glass-bottomed boat at this world-renowned reef site. The best time for snorkelling is at lower tides, when the shallows are better protected and the water is calmer.

On your last evening, the *Reef Endeavour* cruises quietly through the darkness, arriving in Cairns in the early hours and discharging its passengers after breakfast the following day, at about 8am.

Left: trek up to Cook's Look for amazing vistas

3. CAPE YORK PENINSULA *(see map, p56)*

An overnight trip involving a four-wheel-drive exploration of the remote Outback of Cape York Peninsula, including a visit to historic Cooktown and back down the coastal road.

Make an early start and follow the directions in Itinerary 5 (see page 35) to Mareeba, then pick up the route detailed below. You will need an off-road vehicle; contact Sargent Four Wheel Drive Truck Lease and Hire (tel: 07 4032 3361; www.sargent.com.au). Rental formalities include a 20-minute course on the use of your vehicle; make sure no significant rain is forecast, otherwise you will have to miss out on the coastal route. The Royal Automobile Club of Queensland or RACQ (tel: 1300 130 595; www.racq.com.au) can provide useful motoring information. Book a room at Cooktown's Milkwood Lodge Rainforest Retreat (tel: 07 4069 5007; www.milkwoodlodge.com), or rent a four-wheel-drive vehicle with rooftop tent instead. Only informal clothing and swimming gear will be needed. Take some food and drinks in an 'esky' (insulated cooler); ice is sold at most service stations, but these are few and far between in the Outback, so top up with fuel at every opportunity.

On the **Mulligan Highway** (Peninsular Development Road) from Mareeba, it's 185km (115 miles) to Lakeland Downs, and 266km (165 miles) to Cooktown. Here and there you'll see signs warning of 'road trains' – huge trucks with multiple trailers – which take up a great deal of space and are very heavy, with limited manoeuvrability. If you encounter one, pull over as far as you can and give it plenty of room. Locals reckon if they can see three all at once, it's a traffic jam.

This is where the **Outback** really begins. You're quite suddenly in a wide expanse of under-populated

Above: Outback scenery
Right: typical 'road train'

land, some of it cleared for grazing and some open bush with a great diversity of forest types. Much of the landscape is unfenced, so beware of wandering cattle and kangaroos. The latter are most active in the early morning and at dusk when they sometimes emerge from the bush at high speed,

inflicting serious damage on themselves and passing vehicles. There are rest bays near some of the bridges, and in dry weather the streams that are still running attract lots of bird life. You might also see a platypus swimming low in the waters of a quiet billabong.

The rest area at **Rifle Creek** is excellent for a picnic. It is about 2km (1¼ miles) beyond the town on the left, with tall, rustling eucalypts providing shade.

From the road, you'll see the rainforested coastal ranges on the distant right, and barren rocky outcrops on the left. Food and fuel outlets are limited to the isolated townships along the way, and wide open spaces separate the sparse homesteads, which are usually marked only by a dirt driveway and a mailbox. Beyond **Mount Carbine**, once a thriving mining township but now offering little beyond a store, a hotel/motel and a roadhouse, the road sweeps up a steep range to **Bob's Lookout**. Here, you'll get a view of the wilderness that extends to the horizon.

Lakeland Downs and Black Mountain

Some 84km (52 miles) beyond Mount Carbine, the **Palmer River Goldfields Roadhouse** (tel: 07 4060 2020), framed by colourful bougainvillaea and lined with local slate, is a good spot to enjoy a snack. You can also browse the small collection of memorabilia from the Palmer River gold rush, which produced 80 tons of gold before the lode was exhausted.

Over and down the mighty Byerstown Range, you will reach the open plains of **Lakeland Downs**, with a permanent population of about 100 hardy souls. There were once great plans for this settlement, including a vast irrigation project, land clearance for grain crops and a railway to the coast near Cooktown. The project then ran out of cash and the land was divided into small farms, which now grow melons, navy beans, peanuts, pawpaw and bananas. If you're ready for lunch, the **Lakeland Downs Hotel** (noon– 2.30pm; tel: 07 4060 2142) can oblige.

From here, the unsealed road forks left and gets more and more rugged all the way to faraway Cape York, so unless you have a spare week or more, continue straight on the newly sealed 79km (49 miles) road to Cooktown. It was along this approximate route, with diverse landscape playing host to 'vine scrub', which obstructed the early explorers, that the prospectors who survived the Aborigines' vigorous armed resistance to their passage found their way to the goldfields. A causeway and a low bridge take you across the **Little Annan River Gorge**, where debris in the foliage betrays occasional high flood levels. Three kilometres (2 miles) further on, stop at the lookout

Above: wandering cattle are one of the road hazards on the Cooktown route

that commands a view of the amazing **Black Mountain**, which has the appearance of a huge pile of black boulders. It has found a place in Aboriginal and subsequent European legends, mostly surrounding the supposed mysterious disappearance of climbers who entered its dark caverns. A plaque explains the weird formation, and sometimes white cockatoos can be seen silhouetted against it, circling in the thermals rising from the warm rocks.

Captain Cook's Town

Re-crossing the Annan River, this time close to its mouth, you'll enter **Cooktown**, with a population of about 1,600, well down from the 35,000-odd during its gold rush days. The town is named after Captain James Cook who beached his exploration ship *Endeavour* here in 1770 after damaging it on a coral reef. Four-wheel-drive vehicles dominate Main Street. Squadrons of visitors, many of them from the southern states, flock to the Cape York Peninsula every winter to pit their vehicles, equipment and driving skills against the rugged terrain and the bone-shaking bush tracks.

You may have made a reservation at **Milkwood Lodge Rainforest Retreat** *(see page 59)* in Annan Road. If not, and you're equipped for camping, head for the 3-ha (7½-acre) **Cooktown Holiday Park** (tel: 1800 255 162 or 07 4069 5417; www.cooktownholidaypark.com.au) at the junction of Charlotte Street and McIvor Road.

There should be plenty of time after you've checked in to visit the town's historic centrepiece, the **James Cook Historical Museum** (daily 9.30am–4pm; tel: 07 4069 5386) on the corner of Furneaux Street and Helen Street. Occupying an impressive building, it is now administered by the National Trust of Queensland, and among its prized exhibits are a cannon and the anchor from the *Endeavour*, recovered from the reef in 1969.

Above: Black Mountain
Right: James Cook Historical Museum

The **Nature's Powerhouse** in the Botanic Gardens (Walker Street; daily 9am–5pm; admission charge for galleries; tel 07 4069 6004) is also worth a visit. The centre, built of corrugated iron and set in the gardens, features local and travelling exhibitions. If there's time, pause for a munch or lunch at **The Veranda Café**, after which you can take a 650-m (¾-mile) trail through natural bushland to **Finch Bay**. You may see wallabies along the way, and there'll be wild flowers in spring and often a profusion of butterflies in summer. The **Cooktown Cemetery** in McIvor Road contains a **Chinese Shrine** honouring the estimated 20,000 Chinese prospectors who worked in the goldfields, many of whom are buried here.

Before dinner, drive (or walk) up **Grassy Hill** with its old lighthouse, and gaze out across the sweeping coastline and maze of coral reefs, as Cook once did in his search for a safe passage. Watch the sunset, perhaps, and take in a few lungfuls of the clean sea air. Alternatively, if you enjoy fishing you can soak up the evening peace of the jetty. Bait and tackle can be found at the **Lure Shop** at 209 Charlotte Street. As for nightlife – maybe, in a decade or two. Meanwhile, the **Bowling Club** in Charlotte Street (daily 6–9pm; tel: 07 4069 5819) welcomes visitors. Four-wheel-drive tours, river cruises and guided fishing trips are also available.

Cedar Bay and the Coast Road

In the morning, leave by about 10.30am if you intend to return to Cairns by nightfall. But first (if you're not already out there fishing), stroll along the **Esplanade** to the wharf and have breakfast at **Cook's Landing Kiosk** (daily 7am–4pm; tel: 07 4069 5101). On the way, you'll see several monuments, including those honouring Captain Cook and the battling gold miners.

Top up with fuel here, as there's otherwise no guarantee of getting any before you reach Cape Tribulation, and load up with supplies and ice if you want a picnic lunch (though there are places to eat along the way). If you want to visit the **Cedar Bay National Park**, call the National Parks (tel: 07 4069 5777) in Cooktown for an update. Then retrace yesterday's route to the point just past Black Mountain, where a sign directs you left to the famous **Lions Den** pub at Helenvale (www. lionsdenhotel.com.au).

Remember to engage your hubs in four-wheel-drive mode, or you'll discover your mistake at the least opportune moment! The proudly primitive Lions Den pub, built in

Above: lighthouse on Grassy Hill
Left: Lion's Den pub, Cooktown
Right: view of Bloomfield River

1875, is an unsophisticated structure, often peopled by local characters watching the four-wheel-drive procession with quizzical amusement. In the shop at the far end of the pub there are a few souvenirs, including some Aboriginal pieces. A Lion's Den singlet is *de rigueur* for anybody north of the 16th parallel. Good camping facilities are provided in the grounds of the pub.

From here on there's little in the way of civilisation and the road is mostly formed gravel, some of it corrugated, with a few sealed tracts identifying the proximity of homes whose occupants don't enjoy eating dust. Watch out for oncoming traffic along the narrow sections. The road mostly passes through rainforest, and at the Cedar Bay National Park the going gets increasingly rugged. For lunch, stop at the **Croc & Barra Café** (noon–2pm; tel: 07 4060 8125), at the corner of West Street and Third Street, Ayton.

The Coral Coast Road

When you see the **Bloomfield River** on the left, you're approaching the Wujal Wujal Aboriginal community (no visitor facilities) and the road soon takes a sharp left across the **Bloomfield Causeway**. But first, go straight ahead to the **Bloomfield Falls** car park where it's a short walk to the falls. If the causeway is under water (not often but it's tidal), it may still be safe to cross – ask locals for advice. This newest section of the road is very slippery when wet, so drive carefully and give way to vehicles travelling uphill. If you slip off the road, just wait for assistance from one of the frequent four-wheel-drive vehicles that pass by. Although this is called the **Coral Coast Road**, there are only a couple of places along this stretch where you'll catch a glimpse of the sea through the rainforest. Some 62km (38 miles) from the turn-off and 96km (60 miles) from Cooktown, you reach the **Cape Tribulation** section of the **Daintree National Park** and you're back on sealed roads. You should reach Cairns before dark, unless you decide to stay in the area and enjoy some of the attractions detailed in Itinerary 7 *(see page 43)*.

4. THE WHITSUNDAY ISLANDS *(see map, p66)*

The Whitsunday Islands' crystal-clear waters, brilliant white sand beaches with fringing coral reefs, and the interface of reef with verdant tropical rainforest, draw visitors from all over the world to mainland Airlie Beach and, just offshore, an array of diverse tropical islands.

The information here is for visitors from Cairns. If flying from Brisbane, Sydney or Melbourne, just adapt this itinerary as you see fit. Three days is the least possible time you need in the Whitsundays – to justify the travel cost and to savour its attractions. There's plenty to do if you stay for a week or longer. You need to decide on a base: either Airlie Beach on the mainland, Hamilton Island (see page 96 for details of both) or any one of the other islands in the Whitsundays. Note: this itinerary only advises on options in Airlie Beach or Hamilton. Wherever your base is, buy a return flight direct to Hamilton Island with Qantaslink (tel: 131 313; www.qantas.com.au). If driving from Cairns, the 632-km (393-mile) ride along the Bruce Highway to Airlie Beach will take at least 7 hours. Hamilton Island is connected to Shute Harbour on the mainland by a 30-minute ferry ride, from where Airlie Beach is a 10-minute taxi ride away.

The Whitsunday Group

A collection of 74 islands (or more, depending on what sized rock you would describe as an island) strewn in the aquamarine waters of the Great Barrier Reef make up the gorgeous Whitsunday Islands. Most are uninhabited with numerous bays and beaches to explore, and amazing coral reefs to discover. The islands lie on the same tropical latitude as Honolulu in the northern hemisphere, and enjoy year-round warm tropical temperatures averaging about 27.4°C (81°F). The Whitsundays are in fact the tips of mountain peaks submerged in water. After the last Ice Age, the melting of the polar ice caps drowned the valleys between the mountains, creating the network of islands you see today. The waters surrounding the islands are part of the Great Barrier Reef Marine Park.

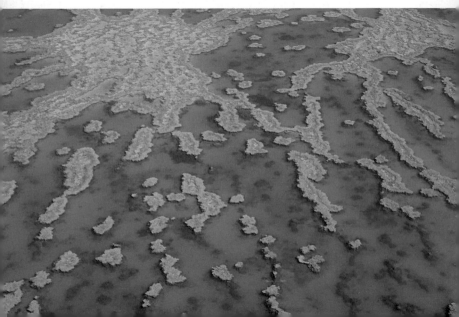

Staying at Hamilton

Hamilton Island (www.hamilton island.com.au) at 750 hectares (1,853 acres) is one of seven islands with resorts – the others are Long, Lindeman, South Molle, Daydream, Hook and Hayman. Hamilton is the only island with its own airport for commercial and charter flights. It is also possible to get to Hamilton Island by sea as it's only 16km (10 miles) southeast of Shute Harbour on the mainland, with six daily Blue Ferry services making the direct trip.

Although privately owned, over 70 percent of Hamilton has been preserved in its natural state so visitors can continue to enjoy the pristine beauty of the island's fabulous beaches, unspoilt nature trails and secluded hideaways. Because it was all built in one go, for the purpose of up-market tourism, Hamilton Island has been described variously as a 'daiquiri Disneyland' or 'a theme park waiting for a theme'. There are several types of accommodation, catering to a range of budgets. Choose from the **Beach Club**, **Reef View Hotel** (refurbished in 2008), **Whitsunday Apartments** and the Palm Bungalows and Terrace. Opened in 2008 is the luxurious, so-called six-star **Qualia**, on a secluded tip of the island. The low-rise **Palm Terrace** is aimed at the 'budget traveller'; it's not cheap, but reasonable deals can be obtained, including packages allowing children to stay and eat free.

There is plenty to keep you occupied: cruises to the Great Barrier Reef, water-skiing, windsurfing, catamaran and yacht sailing, tennis, game fishing, nature walks, whale watching (mid-July to September), scenic flights, safari tours or simply relaxing by one of the six resort pools.

Exploring Hamilton

The best way to explore Hamilton is to hire an electric 'buggy', available by the hour or half-day from two agencies near the marina. These automated machines have a speed limiter set at 20kmh (12mph), but they can tackle Hamilton's steepest hill. The agency will provide a map, but it's impossible to get lost – though some of the residential streets aren't marked on the map, probably because they are signposted 'no buggies'. You should park and walk now and then, just to see how the wealthy holiday home-owners live.

Be sure to drive up **One Tree Hill**, the highest point on the island, for a stunning overview back to Catseye Beach, and over the rest of the Whitsunday Islands. On the way back down hill, take the first left to see the timber **All Saints' Church**. One of Hamilton's lesser-

BARRIER REEF CRUISES_____ Daily.
WHITEHAVEN PICNIC_____ Daily.
SUNSET CRUISE _____ Daily.
FISHING TRIP _____ Daily.
DIVE & SNORKEL _____ Daily.

Left: aerial view of the coral reef in the Whitsundays.
Above: lunch at Toucan Tango. **Right:** activity board.

known industries is arranging weddings. Trade can be brisk, especially during Japanese springtime.

Hamilton's shops and boutiques are worth browsing, but the prices reflect the fact that retailers have to pay high rents to the conglomerate that owns the island.

In the evening, soak up the atmosphere around the marina village and see which of the 10 restaurants takes your fancy. Overlooking the marina is **The Steak House** (tel: 07 4946 8019), a good mid-priced option with juicy sizzling steaks cooked any way you like. The **Beach House Restaurant** (tel: 07 4946 8580) serves modern Australian cuisine using first-class local produce; while the more casual **Toucan Tango Café** (tel: 07 4946 8562) is great for families.

South Molle Island

For those lacking the wherewithal to stay on Hamilton Island, a fun alternative is the new **Koala Adventure Island Resort** (tel: 1800 466 444; www. southmolleisland.com.au) on South Molle Island, just offshore from Shute Harbour. This up-market backpacker (or 'flashpacker') joint offers budget twin rooms and quad-share dormitories. Free transfers from Hamilton Island airport or Abel Point Marina at Airlie Beach are offered.

Staying at Airlie Beach

Many people stay at **Airlie Beach** on the mainland because accommodation is cheaper and there is a reasonably good selection of restaurants and shops. Some visitors divide their time between Airlie and one of the island resorts. Unfortunately, Airlie has no real beach, only a narrow strip of sand that becomes a rocky mudflat at low tide. To compensate, a sprawling arti-

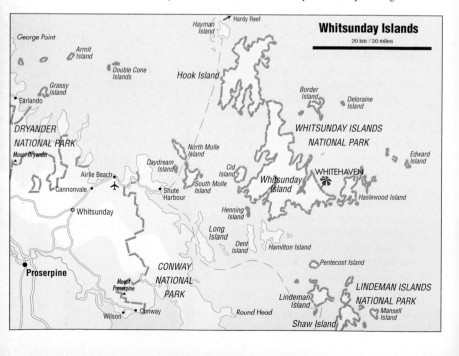

ficial lagoon has been built in landscaped gardens. Airlie Beach is a 10-minute drive from Shute Harbour, where boats leave for various islands as well as on snorkel and dive trips to the Great Barrier Reef. Day and overnight trips also depart from Abel Point Marina, a 5-minute walk along the scenic boardwalk from the town centre. In peak season, a lively mix of visitors swells the population of 3,000, including backpackers, diving enthusiasts and the yachting fraternity – but they haven't entirely robbed Airlie of its charm.

Cruise to Reefworld

One thing visitors should not miss – whether staying at Airlie, Hamilton or any of the other islands – is a catamaran day trip to **Reefworld** by **Fantasea Cruises** (tel: 07 4946 5811; www.fantasea.com.au). Fantasea also operates the ferries that service Shute Harbour and the various Whitsunday Islands. Snorkelling gear is provided on the cruise; if you intend to dive, be sure to bring your dive certificate. You have two choices for the journey to Reefworld – catamaran both ways, or helicopter out and catamaran back. Naturally the second is the more expensive option, but it does offer a dazzling half-hour scenic overview of the Whitsundays, including the world famous Heart Reef, a stunning, natural composition of coral in the shape of a heart. Whichever route you take, you'll have marvellous views of the islands. If you've chosen the catamaran, it departs Shute Harbour at 8am (bus pick-ups from Airlie Beach are included) and picks up passengers from Hamilton Island at 8.40am.

Reefworld is the name of the huge floating pontoon at **Hardy Reef**, which provides a base for snorkelling, diving and underwater viewing from semi-submersibles or flat-bottom boats, and is designed to offer everyone a rewarding experience. You can dive, of course, and there's a guided snorkelling tour with a reef interpreter, but if you'd rather stay dry you can view the coral and reef fish from the huge underwater viewing chamber or from a semi-submersible. There are safe swimming enclosures for children, and you can lounge on spacious open sundecks with plenty of shaded areas. Facilities include freshwater showers and changing rooms, and a buffet lunch plus morning and afternoon tea is included in the price.

The catamaran leaves Reefworld at 4.05pm and lands you at Hamilton Island at 4.15pm and Shute Harbour at 5.10pm. And if you love it so much you don't want to leave, Reefworld offers unique accommodation on the Great Barrier Reef with '**Reef-sleep**', enabling visitors to spend the night among the pristine natural environment of the Outer Reef.

Whitehaven Beach

If you're starting from Airlie Beach, book the **Two-Island Cruise** with Fantasea Cruises, which includes **Whitehaven Beach**, the largest of the islands in the group. The ferry departs Shute Habour at 9.35am,

Above Left: sailboat, Hamilton Island
Right: picnic on pristine Whitehaven Beach, Whitsunday Island

arrives on Hamilton at 10.05am and allows passengers about 2½ hours to enjoy the island before picking up Hamilton guests for the trip to Whitehaven Beach – an all-you-can-eat buffet lunch is served on the way. You'll be transferred ashore by the catamaran's landing barge onto one of the world's most perfect beaches, famous for its 6km (4 miles) of glistening white silica sand and sparkling blue water.

Whitehaven is a shallow, safe beach, so long it never seems crowded, despite the number of cruise boats and private vessels that arrive here during peak season. Fantasea staff will set up a beach volleyball net for the energetic, and sell drinks from a cooler (take some change). Departure is at 3.45pm, dropping passengers off at Hamilton before returning to Shute Harbour at 5.10pm. There is also a range of other day trip options from Airlie Beach to Whitehaven, from sailing adventures to ocean rafting.

Bareboat Charters

The Whitsundays are the perfect place to bareboat (sail a boat yourself). No licence is required but it helps if you have had some experience. You get a detailed 2-hour briefing on charts, tide tables and simple navigation instruments. Contact is made on scheduled radio calls twice a day and after-hours assistance is available. You can ask for a skipper to be on board for the first day (extra fee). **Queensland Yacht Charters** (tel: 07 4946 7400; www.yacht charters.com.au) and **Whitsunday Rent-A-Yacht** (tel: 07 4946 9232; www.rentayacht.com.au) are two of the better known bareboat charters.

5. HERON ISLAND *(see pull-out map)*

Stay on a coral island on the Tropic of Capricorn and get close to nature. Learn about the ecosystems of the Great Barrier Reef and experience some of the best diving in the world, plus some land-based attractions.

Book a return flight with Qantas (tel: 131 313; www.qantas.com.au) from Cairns to Gladstone, the mainland jump-off point for Heron Island. Reserve at least three nights at Heron Island (tel: 1800 737 678 or 07 4972 9055; www.heronisland.com). Book either the two-hour ferry or 30-minute helicopter trip to Heron. Depending on what time you arrive, you'll either transfer immediately to the helicopter (no flights after dark) or take a taxi into Gladstone (10 minutes) for an overnight stay (try Metro Hotels and Apartments, 22–24 Roseberry Street, Gladstone; tel: 07 4972 4711; www.metrohotels.com.au) before taking the ferry from the marina at 11am next morning (check-in 10.30am latest). Bear in mind that Heron Island is on Daylight Saving Time (one hour ahead of Australian Eastern Standard Time) all year through. Bring your diving certificate (if you have one), camera, binoculars, beachwear, and smart-casual clothing for evenings.

Before making a decision about how to travel the 72km (45 miles) from Gladstone to Heron Island, bear in mind that the ferry crossing can be choppy enough for there to be seasickness medication permanently on board. The alternative helicopter ride has a baggage limit of 15kg (33lbs) plus one piece of hand luggage, but excess baggage can be transported on the ferry. Stuff that you don't need can be left at the helicopter operator's office or at the Heron Island office at the marina.

Heron Highlights

However you decide to travel, your stay on **Heron Island** will be a unique experience. It is one of the few resorts where you can walk straight from your room to the Great Barrier Reef and look into waters that are teeming with marine life. This was the first coral reef in Australia to be declared a Marine National Park and is now a World Heritage Site. Queensland University operates a **Research Station** on the island and the resort can arrange a tour for you.

There are several categories of accommodation available at Heron Island, from budget-priced cabins to luxury suites, all with a tropical village atmosphere. The rate is inclusive of all meals and some of the talks and activities. At the time of going to press, prices for the five categories of rooms range from AU$374 to AU$608 per person (twin, sharing) per night; the return fares (per adult) cost AU$240 for the ferry and AU$510 for the helicopter.

There is entertainment in the Pandanus Lounge, which has panoramic views of the reef, but above all, this resort is dedicated to learning about

Above Left: Hamilton's Beach Club pool at sunset
Left: aerial view of Hamilton Island. **Above:** Heron Island reef

and caring for its unique environment, and includes talks on the island's ecology. You will find no telephones or TVs here, no rubbish (it's all transported back to the mainland for disposal) and optimum use of recycled materials. For emergencies, a pay phone is available in the reception area.

Seasonal attractions

Though it takes only 30 minutes to walk around the 17-ha (42-acre) island, this beautiful coral cay is a real nature lover's paradise. No matter which month you visit, there is always something interesting to see and experts on hand to explain it all. For instance, between October and May it is Green Turtle time; you can watch these protected species mating, nesting and (from

January) see the thousands of tiny turtles hatch and make a dash across the sand to the sea, a truly amazing sight.

In November or December, for a few nights around the full moon, mass coral spawning occurs and the waters are filled with a spectacular display that resembles fireworks, or an upside-down snowstorm – an utterly unforgettable sight. If you're there between June and September, you are quite likely to see

humpback whales passing by on their annual migration. All year round, the island is home to a huge number of bird species, and its waters teem with 1,200 of the 1,500 species of fish that inhabit the Great Barrier Reef.

Reef activities

Some of Australia's best dive spots – including the world-famous Bommie – are at Heron. There are 21 different sites, all within about 15 minutes of the jetty. The staff and dive instructors at the resort's Marine Centre are a mine of information, and you can book lessons, charters and tours, and hire boats and equipment for diving. Make sure you allow enough hours to explore the reef with all its brilliant coral formations and fabulous fish. And when you run out of daylight hours, you could try a night dive.

As well as swimming and snorkelling, there are many other activities to enjoy, including a guided underwater tour in a semi-submersible, reef fishing, day and overnight guided camping trips to nearby **Wilson Island**, guided reef and island walks, and even star-gazing from the beach (particularly fascinating for visitors from the northern hemisphere). Heron also operates a terrific Kids Junior Ranger programme, which is tailor-made for 7- to 12-year-olds. A variety of hands-on activities are designed to introduce children to caring for ecologically sensitive environments, while having lots of fun.

Check-out time is 10am, but you have the use of the departure lounge (with shower facilities), so that you can enjoy the island to the full until it's time to leave. The ferry departs at 2pm (Heron Island time) and arrives at Gladstone at 3.45pm (standard time), and the airport shuttle will get you to the airport in time for any flight after 4.20pm. If not, you will have to spend another night in Gladstone.

Above: baby Green Turtles hatch between October and May
Right: learning the ropes from mum

Leisure Activities

OUTDOOR ACTIVITIES

This part of Australia is famous for its outdoor activities, particularly scuba diving and snorkelling, and for adventure sports. A good contact point for such activities is **The Adventure Company Australia** (tel: 07 4051 4777; www.adventures.com.au), incorporating **Down Under Cruise & Dive**, which offers a range of one-, two- and three-day nature-based adventures including diving, four-wheel-drive safaris, rafting and ballooning in Far North Queensland.

Learning to Scuba Dive

Of all the ways to enjoy the beauty of the Great Barrier Reef, scuba diving among the corals and the fish remains the ultimate, so don't consign this possibility to the 'too difficult' basket. If you're uncertain or confused by the maze of courses and the apparent complexity of the equipment, try a **Discover Scuba Diving** (quick introductory) course and escorted dive, which is an optional extra on one-day reef tours such as Quicksilver's *(see page 48)*. You only need to be a modestly good swimmer, in reasonable general health and free of conditions such as diabetes, asthma and epilepsy. In just three to four days you can become a qualified diver with the certification to prove it.

Scuba diving in the region is highly organised, and you can trust any of the large number of established operators to deliver quality training, complete safety and a well-earned diver's certificate with loads of fun thrown in as well. The lowest age for a course is 14, and there's no upper age limit, but you need to pass a non-strenuous medical examination. You then do (typically) two days of combined classroom and underwater training in a pool, followed by one or two days of open-water dives under supervision. The course teaches you all about the equipment and its care and use, proper breathing and underwater safety procedures and rules, and leads up to the first level of qualification – the 'open-water diver' certificate.

Before beginning any course, you will need to provide two passport-sized photographs (for your diver's ID) and a medical certificate; the operator can arrange this for you for about AU$50. With your certificate in the kit bag, you can choose from a large range of diving day trips or extended live-aboard cruises. Below is a selection of recommended dive schools – for more, visit www.padi.com.

These provide a range of dive courses as well as organised dive trips. Prices range between AU$300 to AU$600 for courses that include open-water diving on day trips; more expensive courses include on-board accommodation and meals.

Cairns

Deep Sea Divers Den
Tel: 07 4046 7333
www.diversden.com.au

Prodive Cairns
Tel: 07 4031 5255
www.prodivecairns.com

Tusa Dive
Tel: 07 4047 9100
www.tusadive.com

Port Douglas

Undersea Explorer
Tel: 07 4099 5911
www.undersea.com.au

Tech Dive Academy
Tel: 07 4099 3088
www.tech-dive-academy.com

Left: a novice diver takes the plunge
Right: encountering an underwater world

Mission Beach

Calypso Dive
Tel: 07 4068 8432
www.calypsodive.com

Snorkelling

Most snorkelling operators, whether based
in Cairns or Port Douglas, will arrange to
transfer you to the launch-point of the trip.
Apart from snorkelling, most boats also offer
dive options, with special introductory dives
for novices who are not ready to commit to
a certified dive course. A few of the larger
boats also offer glass-bottomed boats and
semi-submersible craft for those who want
to experience the reef without getting wet.

Full-day snorkelling trips which give you
up to five hours on the reef, with visits of
up to three separate reef sites as well as lunch
and hotel pick-up, cost between AU$86 to
AU$190. The larger (and faster) boats with
their own pontoons on the reef normally cost
more.

Cairns

Down Under Dive
Tel: 07 4031 8099 or 1800 079 099
www.downunderdive.com.au
With only 80 passengers, the 19-m (62-ft) MV
Supercat allows for personal service.

Frankland Islands Cruise & Dive
Tel: 07 4031 6300
www.franklandislands.com

A day cruise to a beautiful tropical island off
the beaten path, with bushwalking and
snorkelling. You can even arrange to stay on
the uninhabited Russell Island and camp
overnight (permit required from Queensland
Parks and Wildlife Service, tel: 07 4046 6600).

Ocean Spirit Cruises
Tel: 07 4031 2920 or 1800 644 227
www.oceanspirit.com.au
Offers trips on a large comfortable sailing
catamaran to Michaelmas and Upolu cays.

Port Douglas

Poseidon Outer Reef Cruises
Tel: 07 4099 4772
www.poseidon-cruises.com.au
The 24-m (78-ft) 70-passenger *Poseidon*
visits three outer barrier reef sites. This is one
of the better mid-priced operations.

Quicksilver Connections
Tel: 07 4087 2100
www.quicksilver-cruises.com
Apart from its *Wavepiercer* described on
pages 48–9, Quicksilver also operates four
other vessels to different parts of the reef.

Wavelength
Tel: 07 4099 5031
www.wavelength.com.au
Excellent for first-timers and experienced
snorkellers. Efficient and helpful staff help put
the nervous at ease. Takes a maximum of 30
passengers. Office open 7am–6pm daily.

Hot-air Ballooning

Drifting silently over the Cairns Highlands in the placid early morning air is an awesome experience. It's well worth the early start, which is typically a 4.30am pick-up at your Cairns hotel for a one-hour drive to Mareeba. The crew will have the balloon just about ready when you arrive. You're guaranteed a fine view, because ballooning is only possible in near-calm conditions; and you're usually airborne close to sunrise.

Ballooning is inextricably associated with champagne breakfasts, which are included in the package by all operators. It is also possible to combine the ballooning experience with other adventure activities, such as white-water rafting and skydiving, or with visits to well-known tourist attractions.

Three operators in Cairns offer flights of 30 minutes' or an hour's duration in the Mareeba area, inclusive of pick-up and return to Cairns, and a champagne breakfast.

Champagne Balloon Flights
Tel: 07 4039 9955
www.champagneballoons.com

Hot Air
Tel: 07 4039 3900 or 1800 800 829
www.hotair.com.au
Operates out of Cairns and Port Douglas.

Raging Thunder
Tel: 07 4030 7900
www.ragingthunder.com.au

Tandem Parachuting

It may not seem like it to some, but there's actually a lot of fun in strapping yourself to an experienced skydiver, donning a pair of goggles, leaping out of an aeroplane, and plummeting from 2,500m (8,000ft) or more while admiring the view and wondering when, or if, the parachute's going to open.

This memorable experience attracts thousands of visitors every year, and a typical package includes pick-up and return to your hotel, a safety briefing, a scenic ascent, and the Big Moment. The first part is a free-fall descent for a minute or so, then a more leisurely glide after your sports parachute opens. At the planned destination, a recovery team awaits. Most operators offer 'disembarkation' options from higher altitudes up to about 4,300m (14,000ft) with incremental pricing, and videos recording your few moments of free-fall. Prices are typically around AU\$220 for a jump from 10,000ft (3,048m) and AU\$270 to plummet all the way down from 14,000ft (4,267m).

Cairns

Skydive the Reef Cairns
Tel: 1800 005 006
www.australiaskydive.com
Departs from Cairns airport and recovers you from a drop zone at Edmonton, 12km (7 miles) south.

Cairns Skydiving
Tel: 07 4031 5466 or 1800 444 568
www.jumpthebeach.com
Also flies from Cairns airport and recovers you from a (different) drop zone at Edmonton.

Mission Beach

Skydive Mission Beach
Tel: 07 4052 1822
www.jumpthebeach.com.au
Takes off from Tully airport and lands you on Mission Beach or Dunk Island.

White-water Rafting

Experienced guides raft you down rapidly flowing rivers, graded according to the degree of difficulty, in (usually) full-day expeditions that combine stunning scenery, excitement and an outdoor lunch. The fact that you have to sign a liability release form before you set off indicates a possibility of minor injury, but this usually only happens to people who don't

Left: snorkellers get a feel of the waters from the *Wavepiercer*'s pontoon
Above: hot-air ballooning is an option for those afraid of the water

follow instructions. Rafts carry up to seven passengers in addition to the guide, and prices are typically around AU$88 for a half-day and AU$150 for a full day, including lunch.

Cairns
Raging Thunder
Tel: 07 4030 7900
www.ragingthunder.com.au
Half-day trips on the Barron River (Cairns), day-trips on the Tully River two hours south of Cairns and a full-day sea kayaking adventure on the Great Barrier Reef. The newest adventure is aboard Thunderbolt, a high-speed, shallow-draught vessel that gets you even closer to the reef.

R'n'R White Water Rafting
Tel: 07 4041 9444
www.raft.com.au
Two rafting tours daily – a full day on the Tully River or a half day on the Barron River. You can also helicopter into the North Johnstone River's untouched wilderness.

Bungy Jumping
Australians will tell you that only a New Zealander could dream this up. Hurtling earthwards head-first won't make your eyes pop out, but the rapid reduction from 95kph (59mph) to zero terminal velocity is certainly an experience.

   A J Hackett Bungy (tel: 07 4057 7188; www.ajhackett.com.au) invites you to step into space from its 50-m (164-ft) tower, high in the rainforest, with your heart in your mouth and nothing in your pockets. The tension of the big elastic band can be adjusted so your head dips in the pool below at the end of the fall!

Scenic Flights
Scenic flight operators offer circuits of the coastline to Cape Tribulation, returning via the outer reef. Flights depart from their premises at the general aviation area on the western side of the Cairns airport.

Cairns
Great Barrier Reef Helicopters
Tel: 07 4030 0300
www.sunloverheli.com.au
Provides a range of experiences, some of them packaged with four-wheel-drive and reef experiences and visits to spectacular but otherwise inaccessible areas.

Port Douglas
Skysafari
Tel: 07 4099 3666
www.skysafari.com.au
A great range of helicopter tours, from the reef to the rainforest to outback gold mines.

Sailing
The Cairns Yacht Club (www.cairnsyachtclub.com.au) has a club race every Wednesday and invites visitors along as crew for a modest AU$15, which includes a sausage sizzle and a cold drink. Call 07 4031 2750 after 11am.

Fishing
Anything between dangling a line from a jetty and a full-on endurance battle with the region's black marlin is possible on Queensland's east coast. You can hire tackle and buy bait close to most boat ramps, hire a dinghy in Cairns, or drive to the beaches and coastal headlands to fish.

   For more serious fishing, go with a fully-equipped and knowledgeable guide. While encouraging a 'catch and release' practice, the guide won't object if you take a fish home for dinner; and will even clean it for you.

Cairns
Cairns Reef Charter Services
Tel: 07 4031 4742
www.cairnsreefcharters.com.au

Catcha Crab
Tel: 07 4051 7992
Tony offers you the chance to catch (and eat) your own delicious Queensland mud crab.

Left: seaplane rides for aerial overviews

Didgeridoos, the Aboriginal musical instrument produced from tree branches hollowed out by termites, are also popular. It's said that the average Qantas flight leaving Australia carries enough didgeridoos to start a *corroboree* (Aboriginal ceremonial dance). The didgeridoo (or more properly didjeridu) was designed before overhead lockers were invented, so do check them in with your baggage. The **Tjapukai Aboriginal Gallery**, adjacent to the cultural park, *(see page 33)* is a showplace of authentic Aboriginal art and artefacts.

Art
Helen Wiltshire Gallery
Village Green, Mission Beach
Tel: 07 4068 7280
The all-original artworks on sale are mostly by local North Queensland artists and include paintings, handmade ceramics and jewellery.

The Rainforest Gallery
Gillies Highway, Yungaburra
Tel: 07 4095 2144
The only outlet for 'Rainforest Folk', created by doll-maker Chris Boston. Open daily 8.30am–5pm. *See page 39.*

Peter Lik
www.peterlik.com
Photographer's limited-edition prints sold at the Port Douglas Sunday market.

Books
There's a good selection of books on local history, natural history and rainforest flora and fauna at the **Cairns Museum Gift Shop** (tel: 07 4051 5582) in City Place.

SHOPPING

In parts of North Queensland, you may get the feeling that there's a shop to fit every every customer profile. This keen competition is not a bad thing for bargain-hunters because it holds prices down. Big shopping centres – mostly found in Cairns – which incorporate supermarkets and speciality shops, are home to dozens of the most notable names in Australian retail.

Among the most rewarding shopping is looking for exclusively Australian products (but beware of Chinese and Southeast Asian fakes), and these include timber art, fashion, jewellery, music, art works, leather products and pure wool garments. Cairns is also the T-shirt capital of Australia, emblazoned with humorous images focusing on activities such as drinking beer, sex, or being devoured by crocodiles – fortunately not all on the one shirt.

Aboriginal Artefacts
Some Aboriginal artefacts are 'fair dinkum' (genuine) and some are mass-produced. For the former, try boomerangs, which are always popular. Genuine returning models (as opposed to the strictly ornamental variety) come with instructions on how to throw them properly.

Above: eye-catching bags
Right: stuffed koalas make nice souvenirs

Clothing

Among the most popular Australian clothing lines is **Akubra**, whose famous broad-brimmed felt hats are hugely popular with overseas visitors. You can pick one of these up in Cairns, along with leather bush hats, oilskin coats made famous in the movie *The Man from Snowy River*, and, of course, crocodile-skin products.

The **R M Williams** shop, on the ground level of Orchid Plaza (tel: 07 4051 7000) is known for rugged-looking, highly functional clothing, originally designed by legendary bushman RM Williams, who passed away in 2003 at the age of 95. His products, particularly the well-designed riding boots, became internationally known.

Artist **Ken Done** and his designer wife produce light and bright casual clothes, which are sold at their 4 Spence Street shop in Cairns. **Billabong** at 12 Shields Street has a popular range of Aussie gear for wet-and-wild sports. Lambswool-lined **UGG Boots** are popular with visitors returning to colder climates, and can be found at the **Australian Leather Company** (tel: 07 4051 6711) at 53 The Esplanade. **Weiss Art** produces a range of distinctive and stylish leisure wear, available at most souvenir outlets. If you are interested in crocodile skin products, check out the **Cairns Crocodile Farm**'s retail outlet in Redbank Road (tel: 07 4056 5666).

At **Canterbury** (Shop 4, the Boland Centre, corner of Lake and Spence streets; tel: 07 4031 4783), you can find colourful and interesting men's and women's fashion, including the popular 'Uglies'. These are rugby jerseys made with leftover factory cloth. Each one is unique, and you will almost certainly find one in the colours of your favourite team.

Crafts and Jewellery

Exquisite jewellery pieces are crafted from Queensland's richly coloured boulder opals, lustrous Australian South Sea pearls, and Australian Argyle coloured diamonds, ranging in hues from 'champagne' and 'cognac' to the rarer pinks. Such treasures are best bought from reputable jewellers.

Now that crocodiles and emus are farmed, their by-products are widely available. Handbags, belts, wallets and backscratchers are among the most popular products. Also popular are sheepskin rugs made from the hides of Australia's famous merino sheep. Another speciality are emu eggs – the shells have seven different layers of colour, ranging from dark green to white, and skilful carving produces beautiful intricate patterns.

Duty-free Shopping

Apart from the usual airport outlets, there's the DFS **Galleria** at the corner of Abbott and Spence streets (tel: 07 4031 2446; daily 8.30am–10pm), which is centrally located and provides a free shuttle bus from the major hotels. The outlet houses luxury brand boutiques and local souvenirs. Many goods are available for retail purchase as well as duty free.

Food and Drink

Australian-produced foodstuffs are becoming increasingly popular. These include macadamia nuts, native to Australia and formerly called the Queensland nut. Many outlets sell macadamia nuts in a variety of guises, including chocolates and biscuits. There are also tea and coffee from plantations in Tropical North Queensland, koala-shaped pasta and, for adventurous carnivores, crocodile, shark or emu jerky. If you have become addicted to Tim Tams, Australia's popular chocolate biscuit, be aware that their supermarket price is about half what souvenir shops charge. Australian wine and beer is now available all over the world, but browse around bottle shops for local varieties *(see Eating Out, page 80).*

Natural Remedies

Emu oil, naturally high in Vitamin E and known for its penetrating ability, is popular with massage therapists. It has been

Left: quirky 'Rainforest Folk'

Located at the western end of Shields Street. Open weekdays 9am–5.30pm (until 9pm Thur); weekends 10am–4pm.

Smithfield Shopping Centre
Tel: 07 4038 1006
At the corner of the Cook and Kennedy highways, by the Smithfield roundabout. Trading hours vary. Phone for information or see www.smithfieldcentre.com.au.

Stockland Cairns
537 Mulgrave Road
Tel: 07 4054 3066
Trading hours vary. Phone for information.

Markets
Cairns Night Markets and Food Court
56 Abbott Street through to the Esplanade
Open daily 4.30–11pm. *(See also under 'Eating Out'.)*

Esplanade Markets
Pier, Pierpoint Road
Every Saturday 8am–4pm at Fogarty Park and along the Esplanade.

Kuranda 'Original' Markets
5 Therwine Street, Kuranda
Open Wednesday, Thursday, Friday and Sunday 9am–4pm.

Port Douglas Markets
Anzac Park, Port Douglas
A colourful scene well worthy of 'The Port's' laid-back image. Sunday 8am–1.30pm.

Rusty's Bazaar Market
57–89 Grafton Street, Cairns
Friday 6am–6pm, Saturday and Sunday 6am–2pm.

Souvenirs
Australian Geographic
Upstairs at Cairns Central,
McLeod Street
Tel: 07 4051 4947
'Australiana' gifts, books, music, children's educational toys and outdoor equipment. You can find an Australian gift for everybody back home. Open Monday to Saturday 9am–5.30pm, Thursday until 9pm, Sunday 9am–4pm.

shown to reduce pain, swelling and stiffness in joints; it helps ease sports-related injuries, and some believe it can be useful in regenerating hair growth, but it should be used sparingly.

Goanna salve and goanna oil, despite the names, are manufactured only from native Australian plants, and were first produced in Queensland in 1910 to relieve aches and pains, and were used by Australian soldiers in the trenches in World War I. Tea-tree oil, avocado cream and lanolin (derived from sheep's wool) products, are all designed to ease, soften and soothe the skin, and are a component of a variety of lotions and creams.

Shopping Areas
The main shopping areas in Cairns are:

Cairns CBD
The Central Business District, always known as CBD, is roughly bounded by the Esplanade, Shields, Spence and Grafton streets. There's a lot of variety, from fashion to souvenirs. Shops usually open daily from 9am to 9pm.

Cairns Central
McLeod Street
Tel: 07 4041 4111

Above: a Kuranda market vendor with an array of sharks' teeth

EATING OUT

Australia's gastronomic credentials are born of two factors – the cultural diversity that brought some of the world's most talented cooks here, and the richness and variety of the culinary resources. It includes (according to Australians) the tenderest, juiciest and tastiest steak, the most delicious fish (barramundi, closely followed by coral trout) and an endless variety of fresh and flavourful garden and farm produce.

Some of the best restaurants bear intercontinental names. Without looking far, you'll find American, Australian, British, Chinese, Egyptian, French, German, Greek, Indian, Indonesian, Irish, Italian, Japanese, Latin American, Mexican, Middle Eastern, Spanish, Swiss and Thai restaurants.

Queensland seafood is excellent and usually fresh, but there's also a good selection for meat-lovers (including indigenous varieties such as emu, crocodile and kangaroo), as well as vegetarian options, with superb fresh produce from the tablelands.

Dozens of outlets around Cairns offer good quality take-away food; a popular area is the 2½-km (1¼-mile) Esplanade (called the 'Nard' by locals). 'Fish 'n' Chips 'n' Fourex' (XXXX beer) is a popular combination, and if you have the ingredients, there are free electric barbecues scattered along the shoreline for an impromptu 'barbie'.

Australian Wines

The reputation of Australian wines has now fully matured, and the range is growing every year as more new vineyards spring up. Australia now has more than 2,500 wineries, many offering 'cellar-door' sales. While the biggest 20 companies produce over 95 percent of Australia's total output, 'boutique wineries' make up well over two-thirds of the total number of wineries. A 'boutique' winery is usually defined as one that crushes under 250 tonnes of grapes (or produces under 15,000 cases of wine) a year – but many small wineries produce substantially less than this amount. Check out wine connoisseur James Halliday's column in *The Australian* newspaper – he can help you pick the choicest wine specials.

As a guideline, the best oak-driven reds or whites come from the oldest-established Barossa Valley in South Australia, while the Hunter Valley is highly popular for its fruity Chardonnay and aged Semillons.

The finest red varietals are Cabernet Sauvignon from Coonawarra in the southeast of South Australia, Shiraz from Heathcote in Victoria and Pinot Noir from Tasmania. Rutherglen, in northern Victoria, is known worldwide for its outstanding liqueur muscats.

Many a fine but unlicensed restaurant falls into the BYO (bring your own) category – you buy your wine from a bottle shop and it's decanted for you at the restaurant, although sometimes with a corkage charge.

Beers

Australian beers are famous internationally, and are patriotically consumed in vast quantities by their domestic devotees. The most popular are: Victoria Bitter, a slightly darker than-usual full-strength beer with characteristic maltiness and plenty of flavour; Crown Lager, a creamy, fruity lager; and XXXX Bitter ('Fourex'). Queensland's detractors claim that this name was allocated because few Queenslanders could spell 'beer'. Several varieties of 'boutique' beer are also available, and beer tastings are becoming increasingly popular.

Restaurants

Quality food in Australia is eminently affordable. In the restaurant recommendations below, price ranges for a three-course dinner for two, without wine, are as follows:

$ = below AU$60
$$ = between AU$60–100
$$$ = over AU$100

Above: yummy oysters are best eaten raw

Cairns

There are plenty of alternatives to hotel restaurants (which generally offer dining of a quality closely linked to their room rates), away from most of the backpacker hustle and bustle. Shields Street is known as 'Eats Street', and the Esplanade restaurants provide a tropical backdrop, with more options along the boardwalk at the Pier. Some offer a 25 percent 'early bird' discount (not including drinks) to customers seated before 6.15pm.

Café China

Rydges Plaza Complex, corner of Spence Street and Grafton Street
Tel: 07 4041 2828
Delicious Peking and Cantonese cuisine, dim sum *(yum cha)*, seafood and noodles cooked in a healthy low-fat style. Owner Harry Sou makes sure that diners are well looked after. Open daily for lunch and dinner. *$$*

Cairns Yacht Club

Marina Point
Tel: 07 4031 2750
Unsophisticated and inexpensive Aussie cuisine in informal surroundings, with an emphasis on steak and seafood. As long as your clothing includes footwear, a member will sign you in. The restaurant is best approached on foot because parking is often a problem. Lunch is served noon–2pm, dinner 5.30–8pm. *$*

Donnini's Ciao Italia

Shop 7K, Wharf Street, The Pier Quayside
Tel: 07 4051 1133
Consistently good and value-for-money Italian food, with highlights listed on the daily specials board. A bonus is the great view of activities at the Marina. Friendly, helpful service. Daily for lunch and dinner. *$$*

Faculty of Tourism & Hospitality

Institute of Technical & Further Education Campus, Gatton Street, Manunda
Tel: 07 4042 2664
If you're impressed by the region's culinary diversity, track it to one of its sources. Only available during school terms, this unusual venue provides a chance for well-supervised hospitality students to practise on real live customers. If they appear a little nervous, it's probably exam time. Quite an experience! Lunch only, bookings necessary. *$*

Khin Kao Thai Restaurant

Near corner of Aplin and Grafton streets
Tel: 07 4031 8581
The best Thai restaurant in Cairns is a popular venue indeed. Prices are reasonable, including a daily lunch special. *$$*

Mondo Café Bar & Grill

Hilton Centre, 34 The Esplanade
Tel: 07 4052 6780
Close to the city and with prime waterfront views, this place is also great for coffee amidst palms and poinciana, with mangroves across the water. Its broad ranging menu of international dishes emphasises local produce. The dinner barbecue is especially recommended. Open for lunch noon–2.30pm; dinner 6–10pm. *$$*

Ochre Restaurant

43 Shields Street
Tel: 07 4051 0100
Creative modern Australian cuisine is offered on an inventive menu that uses 40 different native ingredients to enhance dishes such as kangaroo, crocodile, tropical fruit and seafoods. Try the kangaroo sirloin with quandong chilli glaze, and for dessert, wattleseed pavlova with mango sauce. Voted Best Restaurant for 2009 by the Australian Culinary Federation. *$$$*

Raw Prawn

103 The Esplanade
Tel: 07 4031 5400
Peter Horn's menu includes extensive selections of fish and crustacea prepared in Australian styles. Begin with a bloody Mary oyster shooter, followed by a starter of smoked kangaroo, cured crocodile and emu pâté with a Caesar salad; for a main course go for wild barramundi, gulf prawns and Moreton Bay bug meat fried in tempura batter and served with salad and fruit. Open daily 5–10pm. *$$$*

Right: take your pick of fresh seafood

Spicy Bite Indian Restaurant
Corner of Shields Street and The Esplanade
Tel: 07 4041 3700
Since its recent opening, this eclectic Indian restaurant has received rave reviews. Try the house specialities, including Kangaroo Tikka and Crocodile Masala. Open 5pm–late. *$$*

Strait On The Beach
100 Oleander Street, Holloway's Beach
Tel: 07 4055 9616
This beachfront eatery, a 10-minute drive from Cairns CBD, does breakfast and lunch but not dinner, except takeaways Good coffee and croissants for breakfast. Open daily 7.30am–7pm. *$*

Villa Romano Trattoria
Corner of Aplin Street and the Esplanade
Tel: 07 4051 9000
Everything on the menu has an Italian name, including the Carpentaria Gulf prawns and the barramundi, cooked the way only the Italians can. There is also a selection of Japanese dishes. Daily 6.30am–11pm. *$$$*

Palm Cove

Far Horizons
Angsana Resort & Spa, 1 Vievers Road
Tel: 07 4055 3000
Beach frontage with waving coconut palms in attendance lend tropical charm to an innovative menu rich in local produce – fresh local seafood and delicacies from the market gardens of the tablelands. *$$$*

Reef House Restaurant
Sebel Reef House and Spa, 99 Williams Esplanade
Tel: 07 4055 3633
Subtle Asian and Mediterranean flavours enhance seafood, beef and chicken dishes. Start with scorched sea scallop, and have the crispy ocean trout fillet for the main course. Attentive service and an excellent wine list make for a romantic night out. *$$$*

Vivo Bar and Grill
Williams Esplanade
Tel: 07 4059 0944
A waterfront restaurant with contemporary style and fine modern Italian food. Highly recommended is the porcini-rubbed *wagyu* rump *fiorentina*-style, with a rich Cabernet Merlot from the extensive wine list. *$$*

Port Douglas

Bluewater Bistro
Corner of Esplanade and Mowbray Street
Tel: 07 4099 4335
It may seem strange to find a restaurant in a Life Saving Club, but the mixture works very well. The big plus is a patio bar hanging out over Four Mile Beach. Breakfasts, pasta, seafood, and reasonable prices. *$$*

Flames of the Forest
Mowbray River Road
Tel: 07 4099 3144
Gourmet dining in the middle of the rainforest (hotel transfers included). Drinks and

canapés precede a superlative *degustation* menu, eaten at communal tables. Quality wines, topped up generously, are part of the experience – as is a rivetting cultural performance by Kuku Yulanji brothers Bilgamu and Goyu, traditional custodians of the rainforest. The only downside is the price, a hefty $199 per head. *$$$$*

Mango Jam
24 Macrossan Street
Tel: 07 4099 4611
This always busy eatery offers value-for-money meals. It has a wonderful selection of gourmet wood-fired pizzas, many with Asian-inspired toppings, as well as salads, steaks and sandwiches. A family-friendly venue, open daily for lunch and dinner. *$$*

On The Inlet
3 Inlet Street
Tel: 07 4099 5255
'Sunset Special' (3.30–5.30pm) offers oysters or a bucket of prawns while you watch the sun set over the jungle-clad ranges behind Mossman Gorge. The waterfront restaurant then resumes its role as one of the 'Port's' premier restaurants, with a strong emphasis on locally caught seafood. Open daily from noon till late. *$$$*

Re:hab
Shops 3 and 4–18 Macrossan Street
Tel: 07 4099 4677
Serious coffee lovers won't want to miss this always-busy place. House rules include: 'You are only allowed decaf if you provide a medical certificate' and 'If you want skim milk, you are not allowed any cakes or biscuits'. Can you handle that? *$*

Salsa Bar and Grill
26 Wharf Street
Tel: 07 4099 4922
A blend of Pacific rim, Mediterranean and Asian flavours. Tiger prawn and goat cheese empanadas can be followed by fried barramundi with coconut rice. Their famous margaritas go well with the chocolate cointreau soufflé. Open daily, noon–midnight. *$$–$$$*

Cape Tribulation
Whet Restaurant
1 Cape Tribulation Road, Cape Tribulation
Tel: 07 4098 0007
Fine dining comes to Cape Tribulation. Fresh local produce emphasising seafood is cooked Asian-style. An upstairs cinema (with a bar) screening the latest movies is a welcome addition to the Cape Trib scene. *$$–$$$*

Mission Beach
Blarney's by the Beach
10 Wongaling Beach Road
Tel: 07 4068 8472
An up-market spot serving international and modern Australian food. Try crispy roast duck with orange and cointreau sauce or roast rack of lamb. Open Mon–Sat. *$$$*

The Elandra Mission Beach
Explorer Drive, South Mission Beach
Tel: 07 4068 8154
With fine views of Dunk Island, this superlative venue specialises in (but is not limited to) seafood dishes. *$$$*

Airlie Beach
Armada Loungebar & Restaurant
350 Shute Harbour Road
Tel: 07 4948 1600
International-style dishes and modern lounge music, a fine wine list, extravagant cocktails and imported beers. *$$$*

Panache Restaurant and Bar
263 Shute Harbour Road, Airlie Beach
Tel: 07 4946 6337
A beachside restaurant blending Australian produce with Mediterranean flavours. Wines are modestly priced and well-chosen. *$$$*

Left: romantic beachside dining at Reef House Restaurant, Palm Cove
Above: alfresco lunching at the Pier

NIGHTLIFE

Don't look for wall-to-wall sophistication in Northern Queensland. Cairns, Airlie Beach and Mission Beach nightlife focuses on the backpacker party circuit, which revolves around the 'ours-is-louder-than-yours' concept, whether it's indoor nightclubs or open sided pubs. That said, the arts have become respected and valued aspects of the Queensland psyche. Performing arts events range from imported extravaganzas by world-famous entertainers, to happy little (and not so little) local events, at several venues in Cairns, Port Douglas, Kuránda and the Tablelands. The region is also generously endowed with galleries (there is considerable emphasis on indigenous art) and open-air concert venues.

Artistic events are, however, rarely repeat affairs and tend to pop up randomly. To keep apace with what's happening, Arts Nexus, a non-profit-making community arts support association, provides an invaluable service. Their six-weekly quality review (also called *Arts Nexus*) publishes detailed listings of coming events, and can be obtained from their office at 18 City Arcade (Level One upstairs), 78 Grafton Street, Cairns (www.artsnexus.com.au).

Other listings can be found in Friday's *Cairns Post*, which publishes a pull-out guide called *Time Out*, and the *Time Out Gig Guide* which lists the coming week's action and attractions. *Barfly*, an 'alternative' weekly handout found in pubs and clubs, also lists current activities and entertainment.

Above: a Cairns bar scene
Right: beer by the bottle

Cairns

A J Hackett Night Bungy
Tel: 07 4057 7188
www.ajhackett.com.au
Every Friday night, A J Hackett Cairns offers the unique experience of being launched into the night air at the end of a rope. During your free transfer to the rainforest bungy site, you are offered a complimentary Redbull to enhance your exhilaration – or quell your misgivings about this high-energy night. Survivors are returned to Cairns city within two hours to a celebratory party.

Cairns City Place
Tel: 07 4044 3715
Stop by the City Place any time you hear music coming from inside. On Wednesday (noon–2pm) and Friday (7–9pm) you might detect the sounds of the Snake Gully Band or similar local talent.

Cairns Night Zoo
Captain Cook Highway
Tel: 07 4055 3669
www.cairnstropicalzoo.com
Here you can hunt nocturnal animals with a spotlight and enjoy a barbecue dinner and a campfire with billy tea and damper while you're serenaded by an Aussie bush musician. Nightly except Friday and Saturday; bookings essential.

Gilligans Backpackers, Hotel & Resort
57–98 Grafton Street
Tel: 07 4041 6566
www.gilligansbackpackers.com.au
This is a huge, modern backpacker venue offering nightly entertainment, international

acts, a live in-house band, games and quiz nights, some with worthwhile prizes.

Johno's Blues Bar
55 Sheridan Street, Cairns
Tel: 07 4031 5008
www.myspace.com/johnosbluesbar
One of Cairns' most popular nightspots. Local and international artistes entertain from 6pm until closing time, which is very late indeed. Regular cane toad races add some distinctly Far North Queensland-flavoured entertainment. Check out their My Space site, above.

Pullman Hotel Casino
35–41 Wharf Street
Tel: 07 4030 8888
The casino has more than 500 gaming machines and more than 40 tables, as well as four restaurants, four bars, various kinds of live entertainment, and a nightclub.

Ultimate Party
Tel: 07 4041 0332
On any Saturday night, as well as other nights during peak season, you can indulge in an unashamed pub crawl. The price of your party ticket includes a bus cruise and cover charges for two bars and three nightclubs for eight hours of non-stop partying, including a 'free shot' on entry to each venue and a pizza to finish the evening.

Port Douglas
Court House Hotel
Macrossan Street
Tel: 07 4099 5181
The Court House has live entertainment at weekends, a sunset cocktail lounge, and a Wharf Street bistro. 11am–10pm.

Ironbar Restaurant
5 Macrossan Street
Tel: 07 4099 4776
Named after its structure of galvanised but rusty corrugated iron, the architectural emblem of Australian shearing sheds and outhouses, the Iron Bar's classic menu includes indigenous dishes such as crocodile and kangaroo. Entertainment is lively, and the clientele is enthusiastic.

Zinc Port Douglas
U3/53 Macrossan Street
Tel: 07 4099 4419
A cool restaurant by day (try their recommended Cane-cutter's Lunch) this prime corner-spot alfresco establishment becomes a lively lounge bar at night. It opens late every night of the week; until 2am on Friday and Saturday.

Mossman
Karnak Playhouse
Whyanbeel Road
Tel: 07 4098 8111
www.karnakplayhouse.com.au
Unless you're starting from Port Douglas the Karnak is a little out of town, but well worth the trip. The playhouse is owned by former film actress Diane Cilento and her late playwright husband, Anthony Shaffer. A range of plays is presented in a magnificent rainforest amphitheatre, which seats 500. The season runs during the dry period from June to December, with performances on every Wednesday and Saturday night. It's also open during the day for light lunches, made from organic produce grown on-site, and for afternoon tea.

Airlie Beach
In Queensland's backpacker capital, there are several nightclubs to choose from: **The Juice Bar**, which has a 'chill out room' for when you've danced enough; **Paddy's Shenanigans Irish Bar**, which is usually packed and has good live bands on most nights; and **Mama Africa**, with R&B music and a zebra-striped dance floor, all located along Shute Harbour Road.

Right: the rough-and-ready Iron Bar & Restaurant in Port Douglas

CALENDAR OF EVENTS

January/February
On 26 January, a country-wide public holiday marks **Australia Day**.

March/April
Easter weekend: the **Townsville to Dunk Island Race**, a classic blue water yacht race. 25 April: **Anzac Day**, when Australian military history is commemorated with dawn services and street parades. Call the Returned Servicemen's League (tel: 07 4051 5804) for information. In late April, the **Mount Garnet Races and Rodeo** are held, offering Outback entertainment (tel: 07 4097 9238).

May
First Monday: Queensland **Labour Day**, followed shortly by **Cairns Tropical Garden Show**, at the Cairns Showgrounds (tel: 07 4051 6699). Towards the end of May the **Port Douglas Reef and Rainforest Festival** (tel: 07 4099 4308 or 1800 603 000; www.carnivale.com.au) is held; from the 4th Friday: the **Babinda Harvest Festival** celebrates the cane harvest.

June
6 June: **Queensland Day** commemorates independence from New South Wales. The week of celebrations includes citizenship ceremonies. 17 June: **Cooktown Discovery Festival** commemorates Captain Cook's landing in 1770 (tel: 07 4069 6004).

Towards the end of the month, in Laura on the Cape York Peninsula, is the biennial **Laura Aboriginal and Islander Dance Festival** (call Quinkan and Regional Cultural Centre on 1300 594 900). Lots of ethnic and tribal costumes and handicraft displays make this festival especially colourful.

Also in the last week of June is the **Hamilton Outrigger Cup** event (tel: 07 4946 9999). Over 1,000 competitors contest the events; the total prize pool for the 42-km (26-mile) marathon is AU$100,000.

July
Early July: A glut of agricultural shows starts with the **Malanda Annual Show**, held over two days at the Malanda Showgrounds (tel: 07 4096 5349). The two-day **Atherton Annual Show** follows (tel: 07 4091 4260); with the **Innisfail Annual Show** (tel: 07 4061 3051) and the three-day **Cairns Annual Show** (tel: 07 4051 6699) in mid- to late-July.

First Fri and Sat: **Kuranda Tropical Roots and World Music Festival**.

In mid-July, enjoy a weekend of cattle station skills at the **Mareeba Rodeo** at Kerribee Park, Mareeba (tel: 07 4092 1583); or watch some top golfers compete in the **Pro-Am Golf** tournament at Paradise Palms (tel: 07 4059 1166).

In late July, the **Cooktown races** provide an outback picnic race day, with amateur riders demonstrating a wide range of skill levels (tel: 07 4069 600

August

Early August: **Cooktown Art Festival** (www.cooktownart.com.au/cooktown_art_ festival.html; tel: 07 4069 5322) is a three-day celebration of art and culture, encompassing exhibitions, workshops, and indigenous rock-painting tours. Third Saturday: the **Great Pyramid Race** at Gordonvale. Around mid-month there's the **Hamilton Island Yacht Race** week (tel: 07 4946 9999). Exciting **Surf Carnivals** continue through August and September at local and regional beaches (tel: 07 4059 1362).

September

First Saturday: **ReggaeTown Festival** (www.reggaetown.com.au) in Tjapukai Cultural Park, Cairns is Australia's only major reggae festival.

First Sunday: the Cairns Botanic Gardens **Spring Festival** (tel: 07 4044 3398).

Festival Cairns takes place in the first three weeks of the month, encompassing the Cairns Amateurs Race Meeting and street parades (tel: 07 4033 7454).

Third Sat and Sun: **Weipa (Cape York) Fest, Land and Sea, You and Me.**

October

First Friday: start of the nine-day **Go Troppo Arts Festival**, Port Douglas.

First Sat: start of two-week **Torimba Festival of the Forest** (at Ravenshoe in the Cairns Highlands), a competitive woodcraft exhibition (tel: 07 4097 7700).

Variable dates: **Opera in the Outback** in an amphitheatre at the **Undara Lava Lodge** (tel: 07 4097 1900; http://undara. com.au/activities/opera-in-the-outback), about four hours' drive southwest of Cairns.

Mid-Oct: the **Indigo Palm Cove Fiesta** hosts **Cuisine of the Cove**, with leading restaurants running street food stalls, and there's a wide array of street music (tel: 07 4055 3901); and the **Aquatic Festival** in Rotary Park, Wongaling Beach, Mission Beach (tel: 07 4068 2288). On unspecified dates is the **Lizard Island Black Marlin Fishing Classic** (tel: 07 4031 4742).

Mid-Oct: **Whitsunday Reef Festival** (tel: 07 4946 5811) blasts off with a fireworks display and ends with a **FantaSea Food Sunday** on the foreshore.

Third Sunday: **Tastes of the Tableland Festival**, Atherton showcases the region's best foods, wines, coffees and talent.

Third Tues: start of the **Crocodile Trophy**: Cairns, Tablelands, Cooktown: a gruelling 10-day mountain-bike rally.

Late October, **Yungaburra Folk Festival** (tel: 07 4095 2702) celebrates music and friendship with concerts at various venues at the Yungaburra Heritage Village.

Fourth Fri, Sat and Sun: **Mission Beach Film Festival**.

November/December

First Tues: Dunk Island's version of the Melbourne Cup, in the form of **horse racing on the beach** (tel: 1800 737 678).

This is also the time for the spectacular **coral spawning**; contact local operators.

Left: Mareeba Rodeo takes place in mid-July
Above: concert audience. **Right:** a Pacific Islander adds local colour

Practical Information

GETTING THERE

By Air

Cairns has regular air links to Auckland, Hong Kong, Kuala Lumpur, Port Moresby, Singapore, Taipei, Fukuoka, Nagoya, Osaka and Tokyo, and frequent flights to Brisbane, Sydney and Melbourne, as well as to tourist destinations like Whitsunday Islands, Darwin, Alice Springs and Ayers Rock.

Published fares are high, but off-peak deals are often better than the 30 percent discount offered to holders of international air tickets. Check with **Qantas** (tel: 131 313; www.qantas.com.au) for connections to the Gold Coast, other state capitals, several Asian destinations, and regional coastal centres. Other competitively priced airlines are **Jetstar Airways** (tel: 131 538; www.jetstar.com.au) and **Virgin Blue** (tel: 136 789; www.virginblue.com.au).

The international and domestic terminals are connected by a 400-m (¼-mile) covered walkway. The airport is 8km (5 miles) from central Cairns. Many hotels provide coach transfers. A cab ride to the central business district costs about AU$15; by a 9-passenger minibus it's AU$24. **Sun Palm**'s Express Coaches (tel: 07 4087 2900; www.sunpalmtransport.com) cost AU$10 to Cairns hotels; **Airport Connection** (tel: 07 4099 5950; www.tripshuttle.com) services Port Douglas, Mission Beach and Cape Tribulation.

By Rail

The Sunlander service (three times weekly) along the coast from Brisbane to Cairns takes about 31½ hours. The faster Tilt Train (twice weekly) takes just over 24 hours. The ride is not particularly scenic (tel: 132 232; www.traveltrain.com.au).

By Road

Brisbane to Cairns is a 20-hour drive, excluding stops; by coach it takes 29 hours; try **McCafferty's Greyhound** (tel: 131 499; www.greyhound.com.au).

Left: fish feeding frenzy
Right: road through Daintree rainforest

TRAVEL ESSENTIALS

When to Visit

There isn't a bad time to visit the Queensland coast. The cooler months, from April to October, are traditionally the busiest season, largely because southern Australians move north to escape their winters. Occasionally, the southeast trade winds build up to 30 knots, making sea conditions choppy to rough inside the reef, but the tour operators know the sheltered spots.

November and December are usually warmer (up to 32°C/90°F) and dry, with excellent boating conditions on calmer seas. The 'wet season', beginning on or around Christmas Day and continuing to the end of March, is the time when waterfalls are at their best and the rainforest really comes alive. You may not want to try some of the itineraries (certainly not the Cooktown to Cape Tribulation road), but most options are still open.

Visas and Passports

Your passport must be valid for at least the duration of your intended stay. All non-Australian citizens, except New Zealanders travelling on New Zealand passports, need a visa to enter Australia. Visas are available from Australian embassies, high commissions and consulates, and an ETA (the equivalent of a Visa) and from travel agents and airlines in most countries. Tourist visas are normally valid for 12 months, and cover as many visits as you like for up to three months at a time. Tourist visa holders are not allowed to work throughout the duration of their stay.

Vaccinations

No vaccinations are necessary for entry into Australia unless you have visited an area infected by yellow fever, cholera or typhoid in the previous 14 days.

Customs

Duty-free allowances change from time to time, so it's best to check the current dutiable goods entitlements on the Australian Customs website (www.customs.gov.au). If in doubt, contact a Customs officer or call 1300 363 263 (Australia only) for information. If overseas, call +61 2 6275 6666 or e-mail: information@customs.gov.au.

Strict quarantine regulations forbid the importation of foods, plants, animals and their by-products. The quarantine period for cats and dogs (including guide-dogs) is six months, with the owner responsible for all costs. Heavy jail penalties apply to the smuggling of drugs of any kind. Visitors are allowed to carry up to three months' supply of prescribed medications, but for larger supplies you should carry a doctor's certificate.

Weather

The weather is usually mild with little rain from early April to late September. October, November and December grow progressively warmer, sometimes with evening thunderstorms, but even then the maximum daily temperature rarely exceeds 34°C (93°F). Most, but not all, of Cairns' average annual rainfall of 1,990mm (78in) occurs during the 'wet season', which usually runs from about Christmas to the end of March. Tropical cyclones are rare and the region is well prepared for them. Cairns enjoys a daily year-round average of 7.4 hours of sunshine.

Clothing

In this tropical climate, dress is informal, and few restaurants and clubs require a jacket and tie, even at dinner. Lightweight clothing is suitable all year round, but bring something warm for cool winter nights. If susceptible to sunstroke and sunburn, wear a broad-brimmed hat and a shirt with collar and sleeves to protect your neck and arms. Bring swimwear, sunscreen with a high Sun Protection Factor (SPF) and sunglasses for the beach.

Electricity

Electrical power is 240/250v AC, 50Hz universal. Most hotels also have outlets for 110v (shavers only). Australian power outlets are an unusual three-pin configuration, but adaptors are readily available in shops and hotels.

Time Differences

Queensland operates on Australian Eastern Standard Time (Greenwich Mean Time minus 10 hours). Daylight saving is not observed in Queensland (except on Heron Island, where it is used all year), but does apply, from different dates, in the other states across three time zones, giving, at worst, up to six differing times across the country.

GETTING ACQUAINTED

Geography

The region covered in this book is the coast, hinterland and offshore islands between Cooktown in the north and Hinchinbrook Island in the south, with excursions to the Whitsunday Passage in Central Queensland and Heron Island further south off the Capricorn Coast.

The Great Dividing Range runs close to the eastern coastline, all the way to Cape York, 800km (500 miles) north of Port Douglas. Vast, sparsely populated tracts of tropical rainforest, savannah, semi-arid plains and desert make up the rest of Queensland, which has a total area of about the combined size of France, Germany, Italy and Spain.

Government and Economy

Voting in federal and state elections is compulsory for all Australians aged 18 and above. Unlike most state parliaments, Queensland's does not have an upper house, which makes for a very straightforward way of doing things. The state's conservative and labour-orientated parties have always tended to be a little more polarised than their counterparts in other states, which brings extra spice, if not spite, to parliamentary debates. Politics becomes even more colourful at local government level, with the countervailing interests of environmentalists and developers often leading the field in a media spectacle.

Queensland's economy is dependent on the agriculture, natural resource and tourism industries. The state's affluence is a reflection of unusually high levels of both industrial and residential development.

Religion

Most forms of Christianity, along with the Islamic and Jewish faiths, offer places of worship in the larger centres of population. The best reference for these is under 'churches, mosques and temples' in the yellow pages of the telephone directory. The spirituality of the Aborigines is best explored at Tjapukai Aboriginal Culture Park *(see Itinerary 4, page 33)*.

How Not to Offend

Australians are a determinedly independent and non-subservient people. Those who treat them as inferiors are not likely to provoke anger, but they will probably be completely ignored. A friendly, egalitarian and sometimes humorous approach is more likely to establish effective relationships.

Population

Almost two-thirds of Queensland's 3.5 million population live within 100km (60 miles) of Brisbane; the coastal strip north to Port Douglas accounts for the majority of the remainder. North Queensland has a culturally diverse resident population, of which some 7 percent nominate English as their second language.

Italian- and Greek-speaking communities are among the largest European groups, but there are also Croatian, Dutch, German, Polish, Russian, Spanish and Swiss, along with many Asian and various South American language groups. Most speak fluent English, with accents that are not much harder to understand than the broader Australian. There are also growing numbers of South Sea Islanders, including those from Papua New Guinea, the Solomons, Vanuatu, Samoa, Tonga and Fiji as well as New Zealand Maoris.

MONEY MATTERS

Currency

Australia's currency is the dollar (AU$), divided into 100 cents. Notes come in denominations of 5, 10, 20, 50 and 100 dollars, each of which has a distinctly different colour. Coins are in denominations of 5, 10, 20 and 50 cents (silver-coloured), and one and two dollars (bronze-coloured). The one dollar coin is, confusingly, larger than the two. Shopkeepers usually round up change to the nearest five cents.

Credit Cards

Most establishments display a list of the credit cards they will accept, usually including MasterCard, Visa, Amex, Diners and JCB. Within Australia, 24-hour credit card help numbers are as follows:

Amex: tel: 1300 363 614
Diners Club: tel: 1300 360 060
JCB: (Japanese; Mon–Fri 9am–5pm) tel: 02 9247 6399
Mastercard: tel: 1800 120 113
Visa: tel: 1800 621 199

Left: sunning their buns on Four Mile Beach, Port Douglas

Cash Machines

Most banks have cash machines (ATMs).

Tipping

Tipping is not customary even for taxi drivers and restaurant staff, but it's not unusual to reward good service with a gratuity of up to 10 percent of the bill. Hotel staff do not solicit or expect tips, but won't be offended by one.

Taxes

The Australian government collects a 10 percent goods and services tax (GST) on virtually all retail sales. Under a 'tourist refund scheme', the GST on goods valued at over AU$300, bought from the same shop within the previous 30 days and carried as hand luggage, can be recovered at the point of exit – as long as you have retained the tax invoice. Unlike duty-free goods, items purchased under this scheme may be used while you are still in Australia; duty-free purchases are sealed at the shop and must remain so until you depart *(see Shopping, page 78)*.

Money Changers

The banks and major retail outlets will change travellers' cheques, and many hotels will change foreign currency at a slight premium. All international airports, banks and currency exchanges will change most common overseas currencies. If you're changing large amounts, banks usually give the best rates. Traveller's cheques in Australian dollars can be spent like cash in some outlets, but you may need to show your passport.

GETTING AROUND

Taxis

Taxis showing a light can be flagged down from the kerb. Rates per kilometre are around

AU$1. A small phone booking fee is charged, and most cabs take credit cards. Taxis normally carry only four passengers, but 'maxi-cabs', which take up to 10 passengers, are available on request at 1½ times normal rates.
Cairns Black & White Cabs: tel: 131 008 (this number can be used to call a taxi just about anywhere in Australia).
Port Douglas Taxis: tel: 07 4099 5345
Mission Beach Taxi: tel: 07 4068 8155

Buses

For bus transport from Cairns airport to your hotel, see page 89. Cairns' suburban **Sunbus** system (tel: 07 4057 7411; www.sunbus. com.au) may be of use if your accommodation is near one of its routes. Catch buses at the Lake Street Plaza bus station. Sunbus also runs regular services linking Cairns and the northern beaches. **Whitecars Coaches** (tel: 07 4091 1855) links Cairns, Kuranda and the Tablelands with a regular service. **Coral Reef Coaches** (tel: 07 4098 2800; www.coralreefcoaches.com.au) services the hinterland and coastal centres from Cairns, Port Douglas and Cape Tribulation. **Tropic Wings** provides bus tours (tel: 07 4035 3555; www.tropicwings.com.au). **Country Road Coachlines** (tel: 07 4045 2794) provide services to Cooktown and Karumba.

Car Hire

International car-hire companies offer good discounts on pre-booked hires, with the option to return the vehicle to another major centre at no extra charge. The minimum age for hiring a car is 18, but drivers under 25 are levied a surcharge. A national driving licence is acceptable if it is written in English; otherwise you should obtain an international drivers' licence. If your picture ID is not on the licence, you may have to produce your passport.

Insurance on conventional rental cars is invalid on unsealed roads, but most hire companies insure four-wheel-drive vehicles for any road that is shown on a map. Cover for single-vehicle accidents is subject to a high excess payment.

Driving is relatively easy because the main thoroughfares are wide and well-signposted. Note that Australians drive on the left.

Left: fish on wheels

HOURS & HOLIDAYS

Business Hours

Retailers enjoy flexible trading hours, especially in tourist shopping precincts. Outside the core business centres (Mon–Thur 9am–5.30pm, Fri till 9pm in the cities: Sat 9am–1pm), traders tend to follow the demand, and hours vary widely. Banks are open weekdays 9.30am–4pm, except Friday, when they close at 5pm.

Public Holidays

1 Jan – New Year's Day
26 Jan – Australia Day
Mar/Apr – Easter weekend
25 April – Anzac Day
1st Mon in May – Labour Day
2nd Mon in June – Queen's Birthday
25 Dec – Christmas Day
26 Dec – Boxing Day

ACCOMMODATION

There's a huge number and range of places to stay, and you are unlikely to have difficulty finding accommodation unless there's a major event in progress. Information centres, including the airport accommodation desks, provide free guides. AAA Tourism, the national tourism body of the Australian state motoring organisations, administers a star-rating scheme (one for basic, up to five for luxury) covering all types of accommodation; information is available from any RACQ (Royal Automobile Club of Queensland) office (www.racq.com.au).

When booking, ask for weekend rates and standby rates – it's always worth asking about 'specials'. Specify your needs when booking, and if in doubt, ask to inspect a room before you make your decision.

Resorts are hotel complexes that offer a variety of accommodation and on-site facilities; at the other end of the scale are backpacker hostels, some of which have become very up-market, and camping and caravan sites. The big trend in Cairns and Port Douglas is towards self-contained, self-catering apartments; a number of these are listed here.

The following places have been chosen because of their good reputation. The costs

per night, for two sharing a twin room, accommodation only, are listed under the following price bands:

$ = *below AU$60*
$$ = *AU$60–120*
$$$ = *AU$120–250*
$$$$ = *above AU$250*

Cairns

Mantra Esplanade and Resort
53–57 Esplanade
Tel: 07 4046 4141
Under new management this establishment offers both hotel rooms and de luxe suites. $$$$

Shangri-La Hotel, the Marina, Cairns
Pierpoint Road
Tel: 07 4031 1411
www.shangri-la.com/cairns
Formerly the Radisson Plaza and fronting Marlin Marina and the inlet, this hotel has great views and a great location. Luxury accommodation with private balconies or patios and a range of leisure facilities, including a large swimming pool in more than an acre of lush tropical gardens. $$$$

Galvins Edge Hill B&B
61 Walsh Street
Tel: 07 4032 1308
www.cairns.aust.com/galvins
Genuine old 'Queenslander' in a peaceful location. The accommodation has two bedrooms, a bathroom, lounge and breakfast room that opens onto the natural-rock swimming pool. Only one family or group is booked at a time, so you have the whole place to yourselves. $$$

Above: Shangri-La Cairns

Acacia Court Hotel

223–227 The Esplanade
Tel: 07 4051 5011
Rooms have queen-size beds, en suite bath or shower rooms, and balconies with ocean or mountain views. There are also cheaper motel-style rooms. It's just 2km (1¼ miles) from the city centre, a pleasant walk along the Esplanade. The famous Charlie's all-you-can-eat buffet is available every night. $$–$$$

Gilligan's Backpackers Hotel & Resort

57-89 Grafton Street
Tel: 07 4041 6566
www.gilligansbackpackers.com.au
Not exclusively for backpackers, or even flashpackers, this resort offers economical dorm beds and twin and double rooms. $$

Palm Cove

Peppers Beach Club & Spa

123 Williams Esplanade
Tel: 07 4059 9200
www.peppers.com.au
Striking new resort designed along contemporary lines and with delightful tropical touches. On the top floor are the most expensive suites with their own glass-encased pools and stunning views of the beach. Large lagoon-style pool surrounded by landscaping to luxuriate in and a lap pool for working out. Tennis courts on site. The Lime and Pepper Restaurant offers 'eccentric cuisine' (their own words), utilising the freshest regional produce. $$$$

Sebel Reef House & Spa

99 Williams Esplanade
Tel: 07 4055 3633
www.reefhouse.com.au
Much-heralded boutique property just opposite the beach at Palm Cove. Its bygone-era Queensland architecture is truly charming, with 69 oversized rooms and suites accented by wooden shutters, terracotta floors, wicker furniture and mosquito nets draped over beds. Lush gardens, a courtyard pool and a delightful restaurant complete the picture. $$$$

Sanctuary Palm Cove

6 Cedar Road
Tel: 07 4059 2200
www.sanctuarypalmcove.com.au
Offers spacious one-, two- and three-bedroom apartments with private balconies. Enjoy its 25-m (82-ft) lap pool, spa, children's pool and barbecue facilities, and make a special point of taking a walk out along Palm Cove Jetty by starlight, followed by a soothing massage. $$$

Port Douglas

Sheraton Mirage Resort

Davidson Street
Tel: 07 4099 5888
www.sheraton.com/portdouglas
A luxury resort on the beach, with over 2ha (5 acres) of saltwater swimming lagoons (that are being upgraded) as well as a freshwater pool, and sports facilities that include a world-class golf course, floodlit tennis courts, gym and health centre. Accommodation is in rooms, suites or villas with up to four bedrooms. $$$$

Hibiscus Gardens Spa Resort

22 Owens Street
Tel: 07 4099 5315
www.hibiscusportdouglas.com.au
In exotic gardens with two pools, this refurbished hotel has a Balinese theme, with

Left: Sheraton Mirage Resort

extensive use of natural wood and terracotta tiling. Accommodation spans motel-style to three-bedroom apartments, some with private spas. Less than five-minutes' walk to the beach and shops. *$$$–$$$$*

Martinique on Macrossan
66 Macrossan Street
Tel: 07 4099 6222
www.martinique.com.au
Only a minute's walk from Four Mile Beach, this 4-star property has 19 comfortable apartments with kitchenettes, free cable TV and a salt-water swimming pool. *$$$*

Mossman
Silky Oaks Lodge
Finlayvale Road, Mossman
Tel: 07 4098 1666
Located some 27km (17 miles) from Port Douglas, this rainforest hideaway lies on the edge of Mossman Gorge, which adjoins Daintree National Park. The 45 treehouses and five river houses have all the creature comforts you need, plus a spa, a restaurant, and rainforest excursions and canoe trips on the Mossman River. Now under new ownership. *$$$$*

Cairns Highlands
Mt Quincan Crater Retreat
Peeramon Road, Yungaburra
Tel: 07 4095 2255
www.mtquincan.com.au
Set in an isolated location on the edge of a small crater, these luxury pole treehouses each have a king-size bed, comfy sofas, wood-burning fireplace, TV and sound system, double shower, laundry and – the ultimate – a double spa bath with a view! Two nights' minimum stay. *$$$*

Chambers Wildlife Rainforest Lodges
Eacham Close, Lake Eacham
Tel: 07 4095 3754
www.rainforest-australia.com
Small but superior accommodation with self-contained one- and five-bedroomed lodges, and a great base to enjoy the wildlife of the region. It has an enthralling choice of solo and guided walks to waterfalls, rainforest scenery, and special facilities for observing nature by night. *$$*

Pond Cottage B&B
844 Tully Falls Road, Ravenshoe
Tel: 07 4097 7189
www.bnbnq.com.au/pondcottage
Platypus, wallabies and possums are amongst the inhabitants you're likely to encounter at David and Anne's secluded private resort, 10km (6 miles) from Ravenshoe in the heart of the Misty Mountains. Breakfast included in the room rate. *$$$*

Cape Tribulation
Cape Tribulation Beach House Resort
Cape Tribulation Road
Tel: 07 4098 0030
www.capetribbeach.com.au
Situated 48km (24 miles) from the ferry terminal, this place provides dormitory and family cabins, located as close to the beach as the National Parks Authority will allow. Swimming pool and bistro/bar, as well as kitchen and laundry facilities. *$–$$$*

Cape Tribulation Resort and Spa
Cape Tribulation Road
Tel: 07 4098 0033
www.voyages.com.au
Set in 100ha (250 acres) of rainforest, with its main building beside the white-sand beach; accommodation is in timber villas, in tranquil natural surroundings. Long list of facilities and attractions including excursions led by trained rainforest guides. Four-wheel-drive tours and outer Great Barrier Reef launch cruises available. *$$$$*

Mission Beach
The Elandra at Mission Beach
Explorer Drive, South Mission Beach
Tel: 07 4068 8154
www.elandraresorts.com

Above: enjoy nature and wildlife at Chambers Wildlife Rainforest Lodges

The views from this resort-style hotel, on the southern headland above Mission Beach, are magnificent. The accommodation is set amidst rainforest rich in wildlife, and it's staggered so that everybody enjoys an elevated ocean and beach view. *$$$–$$$$*

Castaways Resort on Mission Beach
Corner Pacific Parade and Seaview Street
Tel: 07 4068 7444
www.rydges.com
Now under the Rydges brand. Set on a tropical beach, this resort has spacious rooms, one- and two-bedroomed units with kitchenettes, and a split-level penthouse – most with wonderful views. All rooms have balconies. There's a pool, boutique, bar and restaurant, and laundry facilities. *$$$*

Scottys Mission Beach House
167 Reid Road
Tel: 07 4068 8676
www.scottysbeachhouse.com.au
Popular family-run place opposite the beach, offering budget accommodation in either dormitories or motel-style rooms. *$*

Dunk Island
Dunk Island Resort
Tel: 07 4068 8199
www.voyages.com.au
Resort accommodation on a tropical rainforest island. Only a 45-minute trip by ferry from Mission Beach. Rooms range from simple Banfield Units to luxury Bayview Suites. Huge choice of activities, including snorkelling trips, horse riding, nature

walks, watersports, plus a children's club. Rate includes breakfast and dinner. *$$$$*

Cooktown
Seaview Motel
Webber Esplanade
Tel: 07 4069 5377
e-mail: seaviewm@tpg.com.au
Centrally located motel offers a wide range of accommodation: townhouses, motel rooms, self-contained apartments. *$$–$$$*

Pam's Place
Corner of Charlotte and Boundary streets
Tel: 07 4069 5166
Motel rooms and self-contained cabins. Discount for YHA members. *$$*

Airlie Beach
Coral Sea Resort
25 Oceanview Avenue, Airlie Beach
Tel: 07 4964 1300
www.coralsearesort.com
The only absolute waterfront resort in Airlie Beach offers a range of apartment-style suites, most with spa baths, just three minutes' walk from the action. The setting is stunning with a great patio café and bar. *$$$*

Magnums Airlie Beach Hotel
366 Shute Harbour Road, Airlie Beach
Tel: 07 4946 6266
www.magnums.com.au
The most central hostel in Airlie has also won awards for being the friendliest. It offers dormitory, twin share and double accommodation, and the cheapest beer in town. *$*

Whitsunday Islands
Hamilton Island
Tel: 07 4946 9999
www.hamiltonisland.com.au
There is a range of room types on this self-contained island, all of which are expensive. Choose from the exclusive Qualia, The Qualia Beach Club, Reef View Hotel (a seven-storey monstrosity totally out of place in this pristine location), Whitsunday Apartments and the Palm Bungalows and Terrace. Palm Terrace is the cheapest while Qualia is at the other end of the spectrum. There's a staggering range of recreation and dining options. *$$$$*

Above: roomy Palm Bungalow, Hamilton Island

HEALTH AND EMERGENCIES

Hygiene and General Health

Public health regulations are comprehensive and properly enforced, so gastric problems from public eateries are rare, and tap water is perfectly safe to drink. But remember that you are in the tropics and, as well as using a high SPF suncreen, you should drink plenty of water. Be aware of the various dangers that occur in nature and how to deal with them.

Special mention should be made of deadly 'stingers' or box jellyfish, which inhabit the coastal waters of North Queensland from October to May. Stinger attacks cause intense pain and often respiratory and cardiac arrests. During the stinger season, safety nets are erected at the main swimming beaches. Swim only within these nets.

If bitten, the sting can only be neutralised by pouring (not rubbing) vinegar on the area. Vinegar is found in boxes along the beaches by the surf life-saving clubs. Make the affected person lie down, to slow circulation, and call the ambulance service at once.

Note that dengue fever is a *major* problem in North Queensland. Use mosquito repellent at all times, particularly during the rainy season when the disease is at its worst. Indoors, ensure that all flyscreens are intact, and keep hotel flyscreens closed at all times.

Pharmacies

Pharmacies are multi-functional, usually also stocking camera film, cosmetics and toiletries. Their hours vary, but there's a 24-hour pharmacy in Cairns.

Medical/Dental Services

Standards are high. Australia has a reciprocal agreement with the UK, but travellers from elsewhere need travel insurance. Without it, a visit to a doctor will cost at least AU$35 and a stay in hospital will be AU$600 per day (minor treatment for outpatients is free), with ambulances charged by the kilometre. Dentists are expensive.

Crime/Trouble

Take the usual sensible precautions – don't leave valuables unattended or on view in parked cars, and always lock your car. Avoid dark, empty spaces and lonely public toilets at night.

Police

In an emergency, dial 000 for police, fire or ambulance. If you should have a problem, the police are helpful and competent.

COMMUNICATIONS AND NEWS

Post

Post offices are open 9am–5pm, Monday to Friday, with some also open on Saturday mornings. Offices will hold properly addressed mail for visitors. The main post office in Cairns is at 13 Grafton Street; mail for collection there should be addressed with the person's name, followed by: Poste Restante, Cairns Post Shop, Cairns Qld 4870. There are post offices in all the towns, and stamps are also available from souvenir shops, most hotels and motels, and some newsagents.

Telephone

All six-digit numbers beginning with 13 or 1300 are charged at local-call rate: 25 cents from a private phone, 50 cents from a public payphone. Numbers beginning with 1800 are free calls. Note: six-digit 1800 numbers can only be dialled within Australia.

For eight-figure phone numbers, you need to use the 07 area code only if you're dialling from outside Queensland. If calling from overseas, dial Australia's country code 61 followed by 7 (dropping the 0).

Most hotels offer ADSL Broadband and/or wireless internet. There are plenty of public telephones and most take phone cards. All Australian coins can be used in payphones but as they don't give change, it's better to feed in small denominations. Clear instruc-

Right: rustic Cooktown post office

Travellers with Disabilities

Provision for disabled people, including wheelchair ramps and toilets, is comprehensive at all visitor attractions and major hotels. Call the **Disability Information Awareness Line** (DIAL), freecall: 1800 177120 or visit www.disability.qld.gov.au, for a useful booklet, *Accessible Queensland*, and information on other support services.

Children

Children are well catered for, particularly in the resort hotels, and the larger hotels may offer babysitting services. Almost all restaurants and hotel dining rooms have high chairs and children's menus. Under 18s are not allowed in pubs and bars. Various sporting clubs, such as sailing and surfing, are happy to involve young visitors; look up the favoured activity in the *Yellow Pages*.

tions are displayed on the phones in English, with some foreign language information for getting assistance. For Directory Assistance, dial 1223.

The GSM 900 mobile phone system network in Australia is compatible with systems everywhere except Japan and the Americas.

If using a US phone card, the access numbers are as follows: AT&T, tel: 1800 881 011; MCI, tel: 1800 551 111; and Sprint, tel: 1800 881 877.

Internet

Internet cafés are plentiful and cheap. They come and go, and trading hours respond to inadequate local demand, but there is usually one available when you want it. Most hotels and backpacker hostels also offer Internet access.

Media

There is ample national and world news coverage on television in hotels and apartments, and the larger newsagents sell overseas newspapers and periodicals. *The Australian* is the national newspaper, and the major Queensland paper is the Brisbane *Courier Mail*. The local daily is *The Cairns Post*. *Australia Monthly* and *Time* are the most popular current affairs magazines.

Language

Aussie English can sound a little weird to those unused to its distinctive accent and colloquialisms. There are a few words and phrases that might be useful. You will commonly hear beer referred to as 'piss' or 'the amber fluid', or be offered a 'tinny' (can), a 'stubby' (small bottle) or a 'coldie'; a carton of 24 is called a 'slab'. 'Thongs' are flip-flops and 'strides' or 'daks' are trousers. Food is 'tucker', a 'cut lunch' or a 'sanger' is a sandwich, a 'counter lunch' is a pub lunch, 'chook' is chicken, 'flake' is shark meat, 'muddy' is mud crab (a delicacy), 'snag' means sausage, an 'icy pole' is an ice lolly and 'lolly' means any kind of sweets. On the road, 'clicks' means kilometres and 'servo' is a petrol station.

Sport

Sport is a major preoccupation that Australians engage in with great vigour and international success. There are four major football codes: rugby league, rugby union, soccer and Australian-rules football; the last of which is the most popular. Cricket, baseball, basketball, tennis, athletics and golf all have many fans and followers. There are seven golf courses in Cairns and its environs. *(See Leisure Activities, page 73).*

Above: so many hats and so little time

USEFUL ADDRESSES

National Parks Offices

For more information on Queensland's national parks, contact the **Queensland Parks and Wildlife Service** (visitor information centre at 5B Sheridan Street Cairns, open Mon–Fri 8.30am–5pm, tel: 07 4046 6600, www.epa.qld.gov.au. Another useful contact is the **Wet Tropics Management Authority** (www.wettropics.gov.au).

Tourist Offices

Given Queensland's popularity among tourists, it's not surprising that the state is well-served by organisations designed to help visitors. Throughout the region are a number of 'tourist information centres', but some are run by operators with vested interests. The following is a list of the official information centres for the different areas covered in this guide, with websites where available:

Tourism Tropical North Queensland
51 The Esplanade, Cairns 4870
Tel: 07 4051 3588
www.tropicalaustralia.com.au

Atherton Information Centre
Corner Silo and Main roads, Atherton 4883
Tel: 07 4091 4222
www.athertonsc.qld.gov.au

Babinda Information Centre
Munro Street, Babinda 4861
Tel: 07 4067 1008
e-mail: babindainfo@qld.chariot.net.au

Cooktown Visitor Information Centre
P O Box 75, Cooktown 4895
Tel: 07 4069 6004
www.naturespowerhouse.info

Kuranda Visitor Information Centre
P O Box 860, Kuranda 4881
Tel: 07 4093 9311
www.kuranda.org

Mareeba Heritage Museum & Tourist Information Centre
345 Byrnes Street, Mareeba 4880
Tel: 07 4092 5674
www.mareebaheritagecentre.com.au

Mission Beach Tourism Inc
P O Box 266, Mission Beach 4852
Tel: 07 4068 7099
www.missionbeachtourism.com

Port Douglas Tourist Information Centre
(operated by Quicksilver Cruises)
23 Macrossan Street, Port Douglas 4871
Tel: 07 4099 5599
www.pddt.com.au

Ravenshoe Visitor Centre
24 Moore Street, Ravenshoe 4888
Tel: 07 4097 7700
www.ravenshoevisitorcentre.com.au

Tourism Whitsundays
1/5 Carlo Drive, Cannonvale, Qld 4812
Tel: 07 4945 3711
www.whitsundaytourism.com

FURTHER READING

Insight Guide Australia, edited by Jeffery Pike. Background essays, attractions and practical advice, all supported by colour photographs and maps (APA Publications).
A Shorter History of Australia by Geoffrey Blainey (Random House, Australia).
Contemporary Aboriginal Art by Susan McCulloch (Allen & Unwin).
Wildlife of Tropical North Queensland. A comprehensive book, with good photographs (Queensland Museum and Queensland Govt Environmental Protection Agency).
Daintree, Jewel of Tropical North Queensland by Lloyd Nielsen (L Nielsen).
Guide to Sea Fishes of Australia by Rudie H Kuiter, a comprehensive guide (New Holland).
Discover the Great Barrier Reef, one of several books published by The Great Barrier Reef Marine Park Authority.

Right: info centre staff on the move

ACKNOWLEDGEMENTS

Cover	**Photolibrary.com**
Backcover top	**Kevin Hamdorf/APA**
Backcover bottom	**Courtesy of Tjapukai Aboriginal Cultural Park Pty Ltd, Cairns**
Photography	**Kevin Hamdorf/APA and**
Pages 75, 84B	**APA**
14	**Courtesy of Cairns Museum**
2/3, 55, 57, 58	**Courtesy of Captain Cook Cruises**
95	**Courtesy of Chambers Wildlife Rainforest Lodges**
82	**Courtesy of Coral's Restaurant/Sebel Reef House**
7T, 64, 65T/B, 66, 67, 68T/B, 96	**Courtesy of Hamilton Island**
86	**Courtesy of Mareeba District Rodeo Association**
38T	**Courtesy of Mount Uncle Distillery**
54B, 69, 70	**Courtesy of P&O Australia Resorts**
48T, 73	**Courtesy of Quicksilver Connections**
93	**Courtesy of Shangri-La Cairns**
12, 33	**Courtesy of Tjapukai Aboriginal Cultural Park Pty Ltd, Cairns**
6C, 7B, 11, 20, 23, 37T, 76, 78, 80, 84T	**Paul Phelan**
Cartography	**Maria Randell**

INDEX